# TANGANYIKA
# COUNTRY OF MY BIRTH

**Massowia von Prince**

**(Haywood)**

TSL Publications

First published in Great Britain in 2021
By TSL Publications, Rickmansworth



ISBN / 978-1-914245-38-1



Front cover and select photographs by Massow von Prince.

This book is for my family:
Anita, Richard, Janet (†), Ingrid – my children.
Natalie, Sophia, Julia – my grandchildren.

As I remembered and as I saw it,
my varied life, with all the different experiences I had from 1939 to 1960, my family asked me to stop talking and put it down in writing.

**Acknowledgements:**
I would like to thank the various institutions whose staff helped me along my long journey in writing about my life in Tanganyika. The British Library, especially staff in the Map Room and Floor 2 – Science Room; The National Archives, Kew: Oxford Bodleian Library Archives, African section, and helping me with maps. Reading old maps helped me with my memory. Reading University Museum of English Rural Life, in connection with Professor H Bassett and his time spent with my father searching for mineral stones. Pretoria Archives. A big thank you goes to Dr AM Samson for bringing me my father's Internment papers of 1939 to 1947. BUT my greatest gratitude goes to Anne who taught me how to use the archives and how to go about writing my book. Also, introducing me to other Archivists. (Boy! Was it a struggle at first.)

Der Besitzer des ersten Majorats in den deutschen Kolonien Hauptmann von Prince und Gemahlin, Tochter des Herrenhausmitgliedes von Massow, deren Plantage in Usambara in ein Majorat umgewandelt wurde.

Verlobungsbesuch 1895 oo 12.9.1896

Mariane Siems geb. Clauss
* 10.11.1875
+ 2.10.1963

Carl Siems
* 15.11.1868
+ 31.5.1937

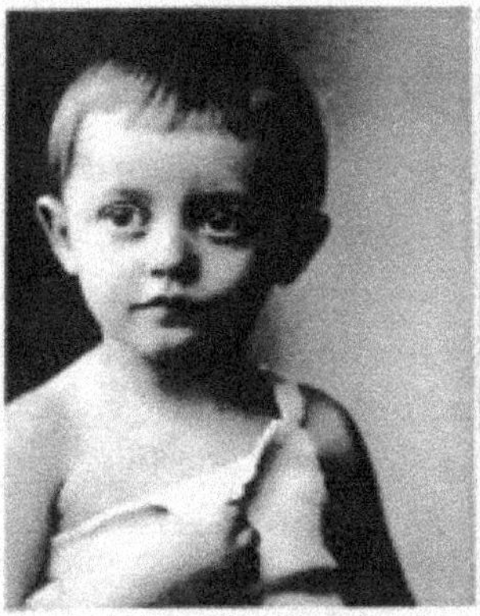

# Introduction to my Parents who first met in Berlin, Germany

In 1937 the marriage of Tom Hans Georg Massow von Prince to Margarete Mariane Seims took place. They married on 5 June 1937, the day of my father's birthday. They had hoped to marry on 31 May 1937, but Margarete's father died that day, and mother's ship was delayed on arrival in Tanga. Massow's brother Adalbert and wife Juliane (parents of Kilulu and Jutta) were there to meet mother. They were there also to witness the marriage at the Magistrates Court, Korogwe.

Before my arrival into this world, the young lovers lived in Kulasi/Magoma and were establishing the sisal estate. The factory had to be built along with various other buildings connected with the factory in Magoma. To help finance this project, Massow took Margarete hunting for elephants in the Umba Steppe. The sale of tusks and elephant skin helped pay the wages for the workers. Mother said the fat from the elephant was good for cooking.

One of the horrors, and excitement, was being charged by a very old elephant bull. After he was shot, they found many bullets and arrow heads embedded in him, also his one tooth had a very big scar. This old warrior must have been in pain for many years. Father gave me these elephant tusks. There was also a charge from a rhinoceros. Juma, our cook, told me he was there for both charges, but stood behind a tree. Father was a good shot. I watched him shoot a crab on the beach from the cliff top in Makindi. Just one shot. He had a good eye.

The rhinoceros horn, when we were living in Makindi south of Tanga, mother used as a good hiding place (until it was stolen one night), along with various other places, to hide her cigarettes. Father used to tell us how unhealthy it was to smoke. Poor Mum, Dad knew all the hiding places.

They made a trip by car to lringa, part of his parents' history. It was also the place his elder brother was laid to rest at the age of eighteen months.

Another time Mother had to cook a meal for their visitors on an open type stove. By three o'clock, her husband came to ask when they would eat lunch. Father took over the cooking. You see Mother never learnt to cook, only to bake biscuits for her father.

Also her sister Irene Szalla, and husband came one time to visit them, before the Second World War.

Mother once mentioned that the life she had with Massow had fully filled her. She could not have lived like her sisters, being a good house wife. She felt she had been given a purpose in life, which I can understand. A lady who had an easy life with her parents came to Africa, not knowing enough English, no Swahili, just her German. Mother then subscribed to the library in Tanga, which sent her books to read, and this helped her learn English.

About two years later, Father was interned on 3 September 1939. Soon after that I was born on 8 September. Mother now had to learn how to run the estate, and complete the building of the factory, plus other buildings, such as the store rooms, workshop and office. In other words, take over from her husband and become a planter. How hard it must have been for her. Not forgetting she had just given birth to me.

I feel I must mention the siblings of my parents:-

Massow's: Hasso, Beowulf, Adalbert. Massow had an elder brother who died in Iringa at the age of 18 months.

Margarete's: Ruth, Otto, Erica, Irene.

I only knew mother's mother – Marianne Emilie Siems nee Claus. Otherwise I did not know either grandparents.

## Ecshe, Clauss and Siems Families

My mother, Margarete Siems – von Prince – mentioned that the Esche family met a Huguenot man who came with their stocking-making machine to Dresden to the Kingdom (or Free State) of Saxony from France in the 17th century. This was during the reigns of Henry IV and Louis XIII when the French Catholic Government was violent against the Protestant Huguenots.

During my stay in 1992 in Germany with Frau Borges, she told me that she was a Huguenot and that the German Kaiser at that time gave the Huguenots land outside Berlin: Limbach-Oberfrohna, area of Zwickau and Chemnitz, Floha-Plaue in Middle Saxony (Mittelsachsen). These areas had a lot of textile mills. In Floha-Plaue, the Siems family had their Tulle Factory.

After the First World War with all the damage done to France, Germany had to pay reparations. So referring to the textile industry, Mother mentioned that the French wanted the metre wide loom, instead of the narrow ones as in the family mills.

Otto, Mother's brother suggested to his father after a trip to California (he was working in the cotton fields) that they ship the machinery to Brazil. Brazil being a Catholic country where the women wear lace veils, the machine would be ideal for the purpose. So Uncle Otto developed the factory inland from Rio de Janeiro in a town called Nova Friburgo in partnership with his father Carl Siems and Julius Arp as a shareholder. The year was January 1925. Carl Ernst Otto Siems mentioned that they had to plant trees for fuel for the factory. In the early years there was no electricity. There was a hospital with staff, including doctors, Club House, and sports area for the staff; also a Fire Brigade.

In 1949 the Russians came to Floha-Plaue and took all the machinery from the factory. Before World War Two there was an uprising and workers went on strike, but Grandfather Carl Siems who always walked to the factory with his workers was never molested, and he was left to carry on working the factory.

The Siems also had other businesses like the forest in Ebnath. Here Ivon von Peterffy, Erica and Ester lived in the Forest House with Grandmother Mariane Emilie Siems, which became part of West Germany. The Russians tried to take the forest too, saying it was part of the textile factory. Also in East Germany there was Schilbach, near Schoneck. There was a collection of trees from other parts of the world. Today (years 2000's) I am told that students come there to study the trees. Other family land was in Zwickau and Dresden.

**Map showing Great North Road**

Arusha, Lushoto, Kongwa are towns where schools were see page 57 for detail.

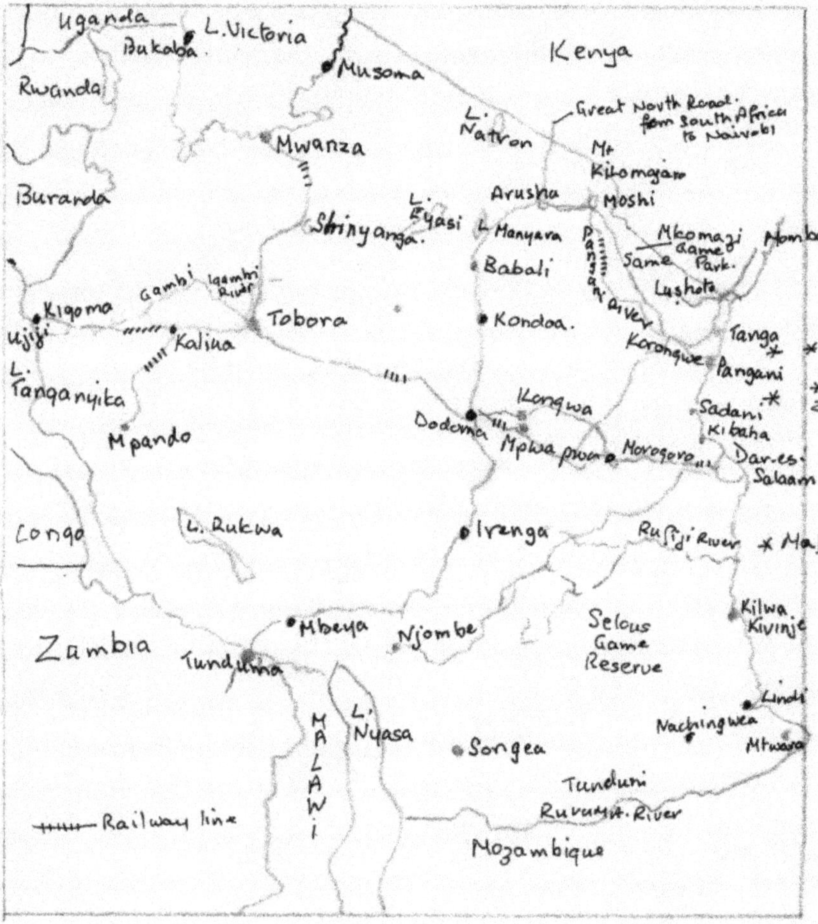

# My Life

## 1939~1960, Tanganyika

I was born in 1939 in Bumbuli at a Lutherian Mission – Usambara Mountains – Tanganyika (now Tanzania). We lived on a sisal estate in Kilusa and Magoma in the Korogwe region in the north-east along the Lwengera valley and river, which flowed into the Pangani River.

Aunt May (Mary) von dem Bussche-Lohe, lived in Kalange with Uncle Willie. Mother said Aunt Emily lived until I was two years old.

Crops grown in Kalange were chillis (*pilpili*) – small red capsicuni – and coffee. Aunt May also kept pigs.

In the house there was a small room, like a little library, and here we played games such as dominoes and draughts.

The play area had a log seesaw by the bamboo forest. In this same area was Uncle Willie's grave, a large concrete like box, with a Wandering Jew plant (*Tradescantia zebrine*) growing.

I was carried to Aunty May in a hammock with cushions by four black Africans. One time I walked up to Kulasi, I must have been about five years old as I was fed up with waiting (see later).

Mother mentioned that at the age of four years I fell into a galvanized bath tub full of chillis and Aunt May forbid me to cry. The brain is a wonderful place to store things. Years later I saw this vision of me trying to get out of the tub. Oh well!

Christmas at Kalange, there was a very tall fir tree near the fire place. Christmas gifts were placed at the Christmas table: under the serviette were little wooden toys. I asked Mother before she passed away what happened to the toys, and her reply was that Aunt May sold them.

I remember the curing room where the dead pigs were hung, which was near the kitchen. I used to feed the pigs and the chickens on a fine Mexican small white petal yellow flower known as Shaggy Soldier (*Galinsoga quadrira*). This plant was used to make tea when we had a cold.

Avocado pear trees grew near the dining room. The fruits were very small with a very glossy deep purple skin, which I loved. I was given sugar to eat with the avocado and I still love it to this day, more than salt and pepper which I do not like.

From the games room I could see a yellow rose at the very end of the garden and that has stayed with me all my life as a guiding star to distract me when visiting dentists or anything where I feel I must block the mind.

## My Parents

My father, Tom Hans Georg Massow von Prince was born on 5 June 1900 in Berlin. As the story goes, his mother was enjoying herself too much with dancing when he decided he had enough of all the enjoyment and wanted to join this world of ours. So off to hospital for the birth of the little boy, my father. Aged two Massow was taken by his grandparents to East Africa to join his parents. Massow and his three brothers returned to Pamerania in 1913 to attend school and in 1917 he joined the German Navy in the Baltic. At some point in the early 1930s he joined the underground opposing Hitler, having got married in 1925/6.

Massow's parents were Tom Paul Ansorge Prince, born 9 January 1866 in Port Louis, Mauritius, died 4 November 1914, in Tanga, and Magdalene von Massow born 2 August 1870 Leibnitz, died 1936. They married in Miletsch, Pschetitz, West Bohemia on 4 January 1896. Both were of military families.

Tom with his sisters, when they were orphaned, moved from Mauritius with their grandparents, Reverend Paul Gotthold Ansorge and his wife to Lenitz, Germany.

Magdalene, once she had clapped eyes on this handsome young man, made up her mind to marry him. What I admire in this woman, my grandmother, is that she made a point to learn everything from nursing, photography, bread making, plus any additional knowledge for a life in Africa. Being a General's daughter in the 1800s, one had servants to do all that sort of work in the big homes, as Father once mentioned when he moved to

Germany with his three brothers at the age of 13. He said there was a man whose job was to polish the silver and nothing else and he wore white gloves.

My mother, Margarete Mariane Siem, was born on 3 December 1909 in the Kingdom of Saxony, something Mother loved to inform people of.

Her parents were industrialists, mainly in the textile world. Carl Siems, was born 15 November 1868 and died 31 May 1937. He was known for his collection of exotic trees at the old home in Schilbach, that to this day is a source for study. My grandmother Mariane Claus was born on 10 November 1875 and died on 2 October 1963. Her family laid out parks and built a dam across a river for the town in Floha which was never short of water.

As previously mentioned, my parents lived in Kulasi/Magoma on a sisal estate, while Aunt May and her husband Baron William von dem Bussche-Lohe with Aunt Lilly Carpenter lived up the mountain in Kalange. Mother mentioned that Aunt Lilly had been in a wheelchair from age 18. She passed away when I was two years old.

It was at this time between 1937 and 1939 when they were establishing the estate that dear Mother had to start to learn Swahili and improve her English. Mother mentioned that it was a good time for her, what with the hunting safari or travelling to lringa (to visit the grave of Massow's elder brother who died at the age of 18 months).

Then the rumbling of war started again, and Massow who had been involved with the underground in Germany, left to start a new life in Tanganyika. But his past caught up with him when the Local Authorities came to Kulasi to offer Father protection as they heard the Nazis were still after him. This offer he refused. Anyway the time of my arrival was due and Father took his wife up to Bumbuli at the Lutheran Mission Hospital in the Usambaras on 3 September 1939. On his return to Kulasi the Authorities were there again and this time took Dad to an interment camp in Tanga.

I was born on 8 September 1939 with red hair, reminding Mother of the red squirrels in Germany. What a shock for Mother to have her husband taken away.

## Father's Internment, 1939 ~ 1947

With the Second World War looming there was a lot of movement about the world. Well, Tanganyika Territory was no exception, and with my family being German we did not escape the attention of the British government. As we know, during 1939 there was lots of talk about war about to start, more so in August, which led to war being declared on 1 September 1939.

The Germans in East Africa knew from comments made that they would be interned, and this is what happened to Massow. Massow had once been offered protection from the Nazis living in Tanganyika Territory, which father refused. The officer arrived at the estate in full official uniform. Father at one time worked in the underground in Germany. Mother mentioned Father often slept on park benches with only a tablespoon of cod liver oil as a meal. Massow had a price on his head and the Nazis were looking for him, even to the point of jailing his mother and an uncle. At this time he was living under a false name with a false passport. The organisation he belonged to told him to go back to East Africa in 1936, which he did.

There were at least 3,000 male Germans and Austrians in the private sector in Tanganyika, and a number were known to be Nazi activists. Anyway, on 3 September Father took Mother to the Lutheran Mission Hospital, Bumbuli in the Usambara Mountains, for my arrival into this world.

When Father returned to Kulasi on 3 September 1939, he was met by the authorities and taken to his first internment camp in Tanga. Their good friend Dicky Gilliespie of Masangula Estate, Korogwe District, went to inform Mother of what happened. I was born on 8 September, and about ten days later Mother went to Tanga with me and barged through barracks and presented me to my Father. After six months, Father was allowed home. Only six months later, he was taken away again, but this time it was a trip to South Africa.

To start with, only men were taken to camp, and the women and children allowed to stay at their homes. But later women and children were also shipped with their men. All non-British

Europeans were known as Enemy Aliens. I was known as an Alien when I lived in Zimbabwe with my British Passport in 1960.

On 26 January 1940, Germans were being repatriated to Germany. From Tanga 459 people and 188 from Dar es Salaam, on the SS *Urania* which sailed on a Sunday. This happened to Massow's brother Adalbert, his wife Juliane and their two daughters, Kilulu and Jutta, Other Germans were arriving from the Northern Provence by train to Tanga. The people were all searched before embarking. This also happened in Dar es Salaam.

After receiving the papers of Massow's internment from the Pretoria Archives, South Africa, I have been able to get dates of movement, and of places and camps. Also some correspondence that Father wrote to the Authorities and his wife Margarete. All these were censored, all the letters were typed and ended, "Your grateful M.", but the odd one had his own hand writing. In one letter to Mother I noted that my name was misspelt, "little Maseruria" instead Massowia. Father's hand writing could be difficult as he had the old German style of writing. You see, all these letter were typed by someone. I must mention that I never ever saw letters written by Mother to Father.

Well! The first document to be signed by Massow in Leeuwkop Camp near Pretoria was 12 July 1940, and on this document Dad wrote: Date of internment 3-9-1939, which was crossed and the dated was written 12-7-1940. How he got to Leeuwkop from Tanga, or what ship he was on, I have not been able to find out. Massow's internment number was 1450.

His letter to Mother on 25 September 1940 mentioned the loss of their baby William on 19 September 1940 (I wonder if that was William's birth date). In this letter, Father mentioned that he, along with Pohl and Koch, applied to be removed from other Germans, as there was a lot of fighting. A document mentioned that Massow was a non-Nazi. Father once mentioned that the Authorities mixed the non-Nazi with Nazi-thinking people to change the latter's thinking. It seems it did not work.

On 2 April 1941, Father was still in Leeuwkop. The file mentioned his association with other men, that he seemed a trustworthy, but excitable man, and gave a written statement that he was anti-Nazi. I understand he often wrote asking to be returned to Tanganyika as he was only on parole, right from the beginning of September 1939, and in South Africa.

Massow wrote on 2 April 1940 to the District Commission in Korogwe, Tanganyika, that he was willing to pay for his return fare to Tanga. He mentioned his family, his grandfather Paul Prince was Chief of Police in Mauritius. His father Tom was orphaned at the age of 14 years and moved with his sister to Germany with his grandfather Rev. Paul Ansoge who retired from the Church Mission Society in Mauritius, and went to the 'Ritterakademie' school in Liegnitz, a Province of Silesia.

Also mentioned were Tom's sisters: Mrs Louise Carpenter was English, May (Mary), Baroness von dem Bussehe-Lohe and May's husband William, both 74 years. And there was Mother and myself living on the estates of Kalange and Kulasi/Magoma. There were five other people mentioned which included their friend D Gillespie for references for his return to Tanganyika. The Chief Secretary of Tanganyika Territory would not object to Father's release on parole granted on 5 April 1940, if he stayed in the Union of South Africa, but would not have him return to East Africa. The letter was dated 2 June 1941.

A lot of Massow's friends were protesting at being kept with the Nazis in a letter dated 16 June 1941 sent by W Zonder, explaining how things were.

Next, I read Massow was living at Camp Koffiefontein, Orange Free State (OFS), on 26 January 1942. Again another censor report. He was assessed as a reliable and trustworthy person having been observed for nearly twelve months and the censor was convinced that he was not in favour of the Hitler regime. It must have been hard for people like Father to be in camp with people with opposite thinking.

At Camp Jagersfontein, 31 August 1942, Massow's medical report stated that he was suffering from a very weak irregular heart action, plus a swelling of the face over the malar region. A letter was sent to Tanganyika in favour of action, that they may deem it necessary for him to go home. Father wrote again to the Chief Secretary in Dar es Salaam on 30 August 1942 to return but this was denied, and also reminded him that on 25 October 1939 he was granted parole which was extended to 5 April 1940. He found his parole was binding. With Baron Egbert von Pohl and a list of 14 other internees. I noted HG Stock's name, a man Father used to visit in Moshi when they were back living in Tanganyika again. These people were with Dad in Jagersfontain and Koffiefontein.

In September/December 1943, Koffiefontein was meant to be an Anti-Nazi Camp, though the internees were very depressed due to the camp misunderstanding, once Italy capitulated, which caused friction and fights, so father was transferred to Camp 3. He fought with FS Soire, Father writing that he had lost three teeth.

Juma, who was with Mother on the estates, had a vision that Dad had a fight and lost his teeth, and he would return home with a brown suitcase. It is how it happened. Juma related this to me when Father was with us and I was nine years old.

From 1939 to 1947 Norton, in Southern Rhodesia, was where the women and children were interned. As I understood the story, there was a fire at the school where some of the children and teachers died in 1945, and the men who had families there, were transferred from South Africa to Southern Rhodesia.

Massow and other men who did not have family in Norton were transferred a year later in 1946. It was when I was seven years old that I received a telegram from Mother that Father was coming home. I was at Arusha School and I remember feeling I really had a father. Massow mentioned that when the Royal Family visited Salisbury, the internees were allowed to visit the capital. A girl at Kongwa School told me she used to see my Father sitting by a window looking very sad.

When the internees were waiting with their luggage at Norton Station, Father mentioned one poor chap sat on his luggage, but all of a sudden jumped sky high. He had been stung by a black scorpion and ended up in hospital for about six months. The other thing Father mentioned was that a lot of people took the chance to study. One German studied brewing, and this man after the war opened a brewery making the Chibuku Beer for the locals, which was a thick runny porridge-like drink. The doctors also recommended it as a medicine for certain stomach problems.

Then Massow was issued with a Certificate of Identity on 25 March 1947, which was valid until 25 March 1948. This paper was in Lieu of a Passport. Studying the document was interesting to me, as it gave details of Father having a long face, straight nose, hair and eyes were brown, that he was 47 years old, and was 5ft 7ins tall. There were other various Visas and endorsements for his travel back to Tanganyika.

Massow's first Visa travel document was from 25 March 1947. Then the British Consulate in Beira, Mozambique, 24 April 1947. He arrived in Mombasa, 30 April 1947, then travelled on an African bus to report to Immigration in Tanganyika on his arrival in Tanga. Following this, he took the train to Korogwe.

According to his book, Dad arrived in Korogwe and went and reported to the District Officer, then the Indian Traders gave Father a lift in their lorry to where Mother with me and the Greek were living in the manager's house. It must have been very sad for father to see the man who had managed to get Aunt May who lived in Kalange to sell Kulasi and Magoma to the Greek Tzamburakis. It was easy for Aunt May to sell the land as Mum mentioned she gave money to Aunt May to buy back her British Nationality. This, also meant Dad could not claim the land, as he was still a German.

When Father arrived by lorry, driven by the Indian Traders in Korogwe, I was home on school holidays. We were living in a manager's house by the rubber tree plantation. When the people left to return to Korogwe, I went with Father to the bathroom where he unpacked his brown case and presented me with a teddy bear with a shell stitched on the side with the writing of our family motto "Beware the Bear". Then Mother and Father went off to Kalange and were back a week later. I was left with the Greek at the manager's house. From then on there was no bonding with my Father. This was May 1947 and I was seven years old.

# Kalange – Kulasi – Magoma

We lived on, or by, the foot hills of the Western Usambara Mountains, facing the Eastern Usambara Mountains, partly divided by the Lwengera River, which flows towards Korogwe meeting with the Pangani River. This area was very swampy, full of mosquitoes and malaria. A lot of people contracted Elephantiasis, a parasitic infection carried by mosquitos from one infected person to another.

## Kalange

Up the mountain Aunt May (Mary), sister of Tom von Prince, lived with her second husband Uncle Willie (William), Baron von dem Bussche-Lohe, whom I remembered lying on a couch in the lounge wrapped in fur blankets. He passed away on 10 December 1945. When I visited Aunt May, she would take me to see his grave, a concrete block coved by the Wondering Jew (*Tradescantia pallid*), a lovely purple patented plant.

Also living there was Great Aunt Louisa Carpenter, known as Lilly, sister of May and Tom's mother Mary, who was married to Thomas Prince, Police Superintendent of Mauritius. Both parents died of malaria in Mauritius. The three orphaned children went to Leipzig to live with their retired missionary grandparents, Paul and Luisa Ansorge. Their son, and uncle to the children, was Dr William John Angsorge, the medical doctor and naturalist who wrote the book *Under the African Sun* in 1898. It was May's brother Tom Paul Ansorge Prince who married Magdalene von Massow. Tom being given the von for his work in German East Africa with the *Schutztruppe*.

The form of transport for me was a white hammock with four porters, the type used to carry the Memsaab or Memsahib (white ladies) in the tropics in many of the colonial countries. Well! one day, I got fed up as the porters were enjoying themselves, so I started to walk up the mountain passing some African huts on the way to Kalange. When I reached Kalange I hid behind the bamboo grove where there was a seesaw. It was a long plank with seats on either end on top of a huge round log. When the porters did arrive I stepped into the hammock and they carried me to the veranda at the front of the house to be greeted by Aunt May. I must have been five years old as the picture of what happened is still very clear in my mind. You see we were all very frightened of Aunt May.

I remember some of the layout of the house. From the front veranda you walked straight into the lounge. As you walked in you saw at the end a huge fire place. To my left were a few steps leading up into the dining area, and from the dining area you went into the kitchen with its store rooms. At the very end was the curing room for hanging hams. On the opposite side of the lounge you went into a small room which had book shelves and a desk by the window facing a garden. I always remember the yellow roses at the very end of the garden. It was in this room that we would play draughts, dominoes, and card games. From this room were some steps leading down to the back of the house. My mind is foggy for the steps must have led to the bedrooms and bathroom, but I do not recollect. On the same side, leading from the veranda, was another big room, which you entered from the lounge opposite the dining room, but I never went in there.

What really stood out in my mind, was that outside the dining room and kitchens there grew hug avocado pear trees. And one that I do remember had a very small smooth black velvety skin. It was lovely. Years later I met a Colombian lady who informed me that in her country they grew wild in the forests. I still enjoy having sugar with my avocado. I know you all tell me, 'Ugh'. (PS, my Mauritius friends have told me they eat their avocado with sugar).

It was among these avocado trees that the Gallant Soldier or Shaggy Soldier (*Galinsoga – parviflora/Quadiradeata*) grew. These plants I used to feed the pigs with. I do not know which variety it was, but I do know they had little white/yellow flowers, and when I was not well Aunt May would make a chamomile-like tea from the flowers.

Besides growing vegetables, there was the coffee plantation, also chilli plant fields; which variety of bird's eye chillis (*pilipili hoho*) it was I would not know. These little pilipilis the birds loved. We would put them into the drinking water for the poultry to kill any parasites in the chickens. Or best of all, fill a quarter bottle of sherry with the bird's eye chillis and you would have something like a Tabasco sauce, hot, but just right for flavouring your meal with.

Two Christmases remain very clear to me. Next to the fireplace in the lounge by the steps leading to the dining room was this very tall fir tree with real candles and toys. What I remember most were the lovely small wooden toys under our serviettes on the dining table, but next morning they were all gone. Just before mother passed on I asked her what happened to them, and her reply was, 'Aunt May sold them.' Mother said she was always selling things, like the silver. But Mother bought them back and Aunt May sold them on. Also Mum mentioned what she earned working for the Sisal Estate: Sh400 shillings, Sh200 shillings went to Aunt May.

Not long before Mother passed away in March 2000, she mentioned that when I was four I fell into an aluminium bathtub full of these chillis, and Aunt May forbid me to cry. Dear Ingrid, my daughter, when I visited her in Australia booked me to see her therapist Annee Hall, who practised Bowen Therapy and Energy Healing Bodywork. After a few visits to her rooms I was able to see the vision of myself in the bathtub and Aunt May tell me to get out and not to cry. Mother stepped away. Annee worked on me till in the end I just cried and howled, something I had never done in my life. Poor Ingrid was in the room and all I could do was to ask her forgiveness for our life together.

I do not know when, but mother took me to see Mr WJ Tame's farm in Tanga with all the chickens kept in cages and the lovely horses. Mother would not allow me on the horse. How he is related to Jane Tame who died in 1999 is not known. She took over from Mrs Shale who paid the German askaris their pensions from 1964.

Once I was six years I do not remember going up to Kalange or seeing Aunt May again.

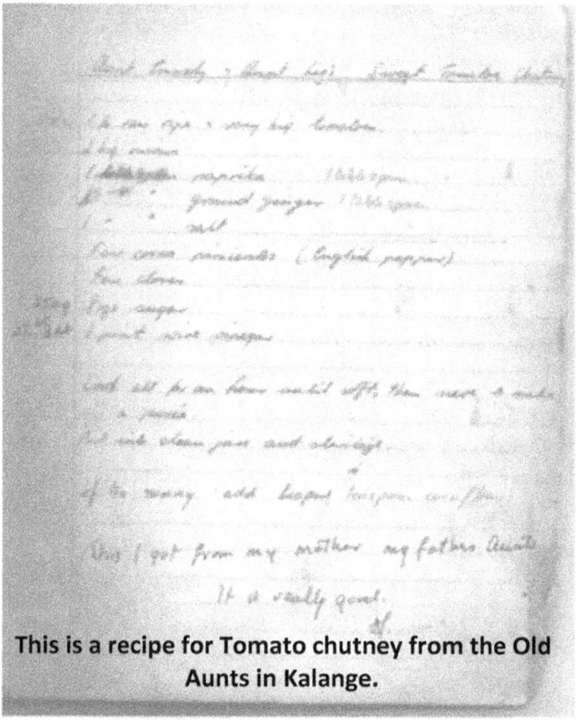

[illegible] paprika [illegible]
[illegible] ground ginger [illegible]
[illegible] salt
[illegible] (English peppers)
[illegible]
This I got from my mother my fathers Aunts
It is really good.

This is a recipe for Tomato chutney from the Old Aunts in Kalange.

Kulasi, with Mother

Kulasi, with Chambo (below); with Juma and rabbit (right) and with a friend (left)

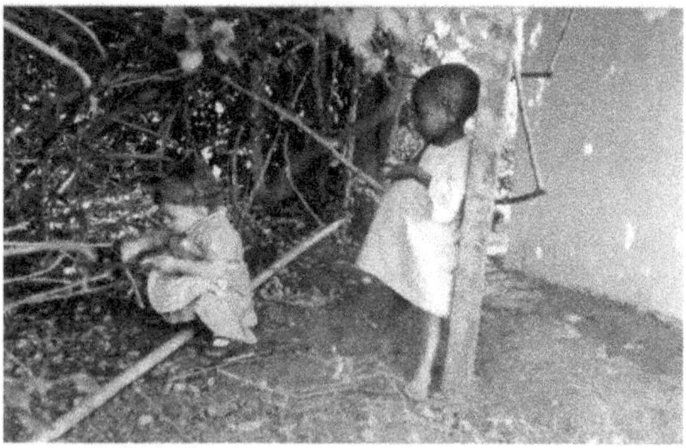

We lived in a lovely open home in Kulasi. Built on the slope of a hill, with a large veranda. I think three sides. The front room had large arched windows with Indian matting as curtains or blinds. The front of the house had a large platform with wide wooden lattice design around it. Below was an open car park.

The inside of the house, as you walked into the open plan lounge, to the left at the end of the room was the entrance from outside. Opposite was a door on the right leading to the bedrooms and bathroom. From the bathroom door or near it (memory is somewhat short) this led to the outside and straight opposite was a large purple bougainvillea, where I remember climbing with Mapera, or Chambo, my playmates.

To the side of the bougainvillea was the outside entertainment, and a big pond. One day, Mother had visitors and we watched the black Africans/staff emptying the water.

Back to the house. The furniture in the lounge was either timber while the chairs were in chrome. Mother once mentioned when she married Father in 1937, Nazi Germany would not allow people to take money out of the country, so she brought furniture with her.

On the left side of the lounge was a book case with a gramophone, the kind you wound the handle, and I used to play the records. A song I loved to sing was *Schlafen mein Kindchen, Schlafen ein.* That is all I remembered, when I was asked by our teacher Mr Casson in Arusha School to sing a song when I was seven or eight years old, that was the only one I knew off by heart. You see the English songs I did not know. Mother loved Chopin's music. I must say, that I also love the piano. We had a Paul Robson record, and when Dad came back from internment I was not allowed to play it, as he said he had become a communist. (Politics!) In another cupboard were board games and cards. I still have these beautiful Skat painted cards. Poor Mum got into trouble when Father returned, she allowed me a free hand into their things and some I damaged. Well Mum was not always there for me. She was busy working on the sisal estate.

One Easter I remember there were the beautifully painted Easter eggs, with bunnies and flowers, stuffed with sweet mixtures, and sweets scattered about the furniture, to the one side of the lounge. What made a big impression on me, was one day I was watching Hossani, our cook making holes on either side of the egg and blowing the contents out. I asked what he was doing, and his reply was that mother needed the shells for something in the factory.

I must mention Hossani was working in the open passage that led between the kitchen house and the main house, when I saw a brown praying mantis that appeared to have an umbrella-like thing over its head. The image is still with me to this day.

Going back to the outside deck, one could look down the slopey hill and see who would be coming. But also towards the distant hills, where there was a lone coconut tree growing. Well once a year Mr Thomas or was it Thomson and Mr Harry Beer (Mother always called him Bill) came visiting, and how could I forget, because they always brought with them a box of chocolates. Mother mentioned they came to check her out as we were interned on the estate. We were allowed once a month to go to Korogwe, our main town to shop and get the wages for the workers. Also we had a trip to Tanga when I was about six. It was my first time to bathe in the sea. Mother had to make arrangements for Father to come back to Tanganyika from South Africa and Southern Rhodesia.

As the local African boys were my main playmates, we often made things like kites from reeds and paper (we even managed to get them to fly) or bow and arrows. This activity took place down by the river that divided Kulasi and Magoma. Otherwise it was around the chickens and rabbits. Working in the vegetable gardens, I had my own little hoe. I liked working in the garden. I also had my own wood mortar (*kinu*) and pole for pounding the rice to remove the husk. It was here that we had a very good telephone system from the kitchen. Both areas had a pole, and hanging from it were tins with a small hole, where a string was threaded through and tied to a very small stick. When you heard the clang clang of the tins you answered it to hear the cook (*Pishi*) calling you for food (*chakula*).

When the local women pounded their maize, rice or dried cassava, they often sang. There would be two people who would take it in turns to drop their heavy pole into the *kinu*. Then they would clap their hands when the pole was in the air, or clap their hands behind their backs or above their heads. When done the grain would be put into a semi-flat round basket to winnow (*pepeta*) the chaff off by shaking and tossing in the air, this helped to get rid of the husks. I still can do it to this day. You hold the tray in both hands, but beat the tray with your last fingers placed under the tray while the thumb and index finger helped to support the tray.

One other thing I learnt from my playmates was to make fire using two sticks and some dry leaves and grass. They would sit on the ground and put their foot on the bottom stick to steady it, place the other stick with a sharp end between the hands and on top of the bottom stick, and then start rubbing the straight stick until a spark would start to smoke from the friction of the two woods; it was the time to start adding dry grass right next to the smoke so a spark could catch fire. Another form of fire making was to make a small bow, where you twisted the string around a sharp ended stick, which was placed on the other stick and now you could pull the bow backward and forward until a spark of fire started.

The family friend, Dlcky Gillespie, who lived on his farm Mazangula with his sister, and sometimes his son Dougie would come and visit, Dougie's mother lived in Nairobi. He would also come to us with his nanny. When I was with the Gillespies, Dougie and I had a great time, playing with all sorts of things, especially the gas mask. Another was fishing with his dad. Mr Gillespie came home with a box of frozen shrimps, which were covered in sawdust to hold the ice together.

Dicky Gillespie

Years later when my daughter Anita married in Johannesburg, I cooked the food in Rhodesia. We froze the meats and tea cakes etc and wrapped the food in cling film. When it came to packing, we wrapped the food in newspaper before packing it into a tin trunk with the goods, but I also added sawdust to help keep the food frozen as we had a 700 mile trip to South Africa. We left the farm at midnight, were at the border in Beit Bridge before 7.00 a.m., as requested by the South African border control, and we reached Anita's place at 16.00 hours. She had the freezer working well. We packed the food which was still frozen solid. The old fashioned way of life still works.

It was with the Gillespies that I got bitten in the face by their huge dog. I was later told it was a Great Dane. I had been warned not to go near the dog when it was eating, and as usual I did not listen. So it was a quick trip to the bathroom to have my face washed and a bandage tied around my head from under the chin to the top of my head.

When I got back from the Gillespies, Mother and I were now living in the guest house. I could not understand, but found out years later that Aunt May had sold the estates to the Greeks. Anyway, I kept my six tortoises in the bathroom. Also my black cat Horsey slept with me, until one night she had her kittens at the foot of the bed. A few years later when we moved to Tanga, Horsey was still with us and I took those tortoises with me to Lushoto School when I was six years old.

While at Arusha School, I was seven years old then, Mother nearly died of Blackwater Fever. She did not take her regular dose of quinine as she hated the taste. I must say the Greek looked after Mother and saved her life. Mother mentioned when I was three months old, I also had malaria and she had to drive the 70 odd miles to Korogwe to see the Indian doctor, who gave me a big jab of medicine in my left bottom. To this day I still have that dimple. (Care to look at it?) Mother mentioned when we arrived at the doctor's that I was totally black.

I was born in Bumbuli Hospital, a place in the Western Usambara Mountains. Mother had a lump on her right breast, which was removed and could not feed me, so I had a wet nurse called Fatuma. So I now understand that my first language was Kishamba, and then Swahili. To this day I still only remember, "*Tite Kiya*", Let's go home. I hope the spelling is correct. At around five and a half years I went to the Gillespies to learn English, before going to the Lushoto School. My other *yaya* was called Evelyn. She later became my sister, Frederica's *yaya*.

When I came back from Arusha School, I was seven years then, we were living in the manager's house by the Kapok Plantation.

## Magoma

There were typical African *shambas* growing sugarcane and rice during my time in the Lwengera Valley between the Western and Eastern Usambara Mountains. The sisal estate, Magoma, was on the road from Korogwe leading through to the Umba Steppe.

From the road leading from Kulasi through the forest and rivers one came across an open area where some Africans had their gardens (*shambas*) growing maize, millet, various beans, cow peas, legume Pigeon Pea (*Cajamus Cajan*), cassava, also cotton with yellow flowers.

I heard that Mother's family helped to pay Aunt May for the estates but Aunt May kept the title deeds. Cousin Chris Szalla also informed me that Mother had her own office at the factory in Germany, so the textile business could help should they need a lorry, etc, finances would be on the way. This story was handed down, so?

To establish the sisal estate, Dad took Mother elephant hunting before I was born to enable them to get money to build the factory and pay the labourers. The factory was not completed when Father was taken into internment in September 1939, shortly before I was born.

My beautiful, wonderful German mother, Marianne Margarete, had become a Sisal Planter with little knowledge of English and Kiswahili. Mother mentioned that what helped her learn English was getting books from the Tanga Library. They sent her between seven and ten books at a time, and that helped her to learn English.

A little way from the factory, was the office building with its store rooms. At the back of the building was the path leading to the outdoor toilet where there was a little forest, and by the toilet was this large tree with a huge nest belonging to a large hornbill (*kwernbe*). I remember it being called *Hindohondo*. The path then continued to a little lake.

One day I spent some time with Mother being taken fishing by an African fisherman in his canoe. Once on shore with a fish we later cooked it in a stick frame over an open fire. Still the best way to get a good flavour.

I feel I must add this now, though it happened about 1944. Juma told me when we were in Tanga that Mother had a really terrible time with the workers. The workers went on strike. Also things were getting stolen, and that locks had to be put on all the doors.

Mother had gone to the Gillespies and complained

about the new labour officer as he would not help get the workers back to work; only to discover that he was engaged to Dickie Gillespie's sister, the lady who was to teach me English so I could go to boarding school in Lushoto. Up to then I only spoke Swahili.

At the back of the building were two T-pole stands, placed on either length of the building, where workers would make the rope from the sisal fibre. Women, sitting on the ground with their one leg bent backwards would take two strands or more of fibre (*kamba*), lick their hands, damp their thigh, then holding the string with their left hand, with the right hand start to roll the fibre together, either way until both fibres were joined together to make string. They also kept adding more fibre to create a longer string. When I was with Mother, I would sit with the women making my own string.

The factory was set away from the office building. Bundles of sisal leaves would be brought from the fields, opened up and put on the trolley, one by one to be laid flat, then fed into the decorticator to beat out the flesh of the leaf separating it from the fibre which was then washed in fresh water. The fibre was then taken to where the long hanging wire was suspended on poles with two wires on either end along a whole length of space. It was here that the fibre was put out to dry in the sun. Once dry the sisal was taken to a shed to be combed and graded, then crated to be pressed and tied into bales for selling.

There was a place behind the factory where the sludge waste went. Boy! was the smell bad! This was the wash mixed with the pulp.

Other times I went with Mother, walking through the row of sisal plants watching the workers hoeing the weeds, or others cutting the leaves of the plant and putting them into bundles ready to be taken to the mill.

Mother always wore slacks but even that did not stop her getting stabbed by the sisal thorn. The place was also good, with its dry dusty red soil, to get jiggers making their home in your toes.

Mother mentioned that by the time I was four I knew every African worker by their name. We had different tribes working on the estate. One tribe I remember the most was the Makonde who tattoo their bodies, but mainly their faces. The women would have their upper lip pierced and a wooden disc put in to stretch the lip out. When talking it sounded like "*Madangu madangu*". Funny how one can remember such little things from childhood. These people came from south-east Tanganyika and Mozambique and the Rufigi river area. They were known to be hard workers, and their wives would be out in the fields cutting the sisal leaves. They were known to be very independent people. Their homes were built away from the other compounds.

The local Africans loved *ngomas* or parties, dancing, and drum beating, with singing, and the women ululating with their tongues. The drums were made from hollowed-out tree trunks, and decorated. At the top, animal skin would be stretched over and nailed in place. These long drums would be held between the knees and near a fire. The heat helped the skin increase the tone of the beat. I loved the sound and music. Sometimes these *ngomas* were held at Kulasi by the drive below the house in the evening. Also travelling with the Africans in the lorries, they always seemed to be singing.

When I came back home from Arusha School soon after Mother nearly died of the Blackwater Fever, I found we had been moved to the manager's house where there were rubber and kapok plantations. It was among the trees where I was taken by an African who raped me, I was seven years old. This same man approached me again when I was on the beach with a friend in Makindi, Tanga.

There was a field of large papaya (paw paw) plants, where the workers would tap/cut the green paw paw to extract the latex (milk), which was dried into a papain powder. This was sent to America. After the second year the Americans would not buy the papain as the Greeks had added cornflower to increase the weight of the product. Mother mentioned it had a very good price.

Kapok trees (*Ceibsa pentandra*) had a silky cotton fibre. These tall majestic trees have pods full of silky fibre and seeds. When the green pods turned brown they would bust open, and some would fall to the ground. I still do not know how it was harvested, because a lot of the trees had thick sharp thorns all the way up the trunk. Once the hard shell on the pod was removed, the fibre was put into a 45 gallon drum. The worker had a long stick with two sticks in the shape of a cross attached to one end of the long thin pole. The worker would have used his hands to rub the stick backward and forward which helped to loosen the black seeds from the fibre. There were a lot of the Red Stainer bug (*Dysdercus cingulatus* a member of the Pyrrhocoridau family). They were just everywhere inside and out of those old oil drums. Ugh!

The best bed I ever had was the Indian wooden-framed bed with woven long strips of basket-like· belts across the bottom. Then the mattress was stuffed with Kapok; Mum's lounge cushions were also stuffed with Kapok.

There was a small patch of ground where rubber trees (*Hevea Brasiliensis*) grew. Here, I saw the local Africans cutting bark off the tree into a V shape and a tin attached to the bottom of the V to collect the latex. This sticky liquid was later boiled and formed into a ball, ready for sale.

At eight years old (1947), we were still living in the manger's house, and I just happened to be back on school holiday, when a lorry arrived driven by the Indians from Korogwe who brought my father, recently back from South Africa/Southern Rhodesia. Mother and the Greek were there also. I went with Father to the bathroom where Dad opened his brown leather suitcase and presented me with a teddy bear, which had a shell sawn it with our motto, "Beware the Bear". Then Dad and Mum went off by foot for a week to Aunt May up in Kalange (so it felt). On their return, the Greek complained that I kicked him in the night, as he had me sleeping in the same bed.

Father was trying to get his sisal estate back and I went with him to Kulasi to see the Greek. On our way there we could not go further as the Greek had dug a deep trench right across the road. So we turned back. Poor Dad. It was here that we noticed two snakes trying to swallow each other. Dad just picked up this bundle of snakes to show Mother.

## 1947~1949, Lwengera Valley

The last two years or so were like living in a muddle and not knowing what to expect when I came home from Arusha School.

First was Massow's return from internment camp. Mother and I were living in the manager's house with the Greek.

Next time I was home from school, Father was working for the government building a road up the Usambara Mountain. Where quite, I cannot tell, all I know it was high up, with a lot of going into and out of the valleys. For me it was an interesting time, seeing the workers, setting dynamite to blow up the rocks; once done the road building progressed.

There was always another valley, then moving round to the next "nose" as Father called the jutting out hills going up the mountain. Years later Mother informed me the road was never used.

We were living in big tents, real safari style. One of my enduring images is the African cook, cooking in his open kitchen shelter.

What I remember most was the cylinder with an auger and handle, which was turned to roast the coffee beans. This was placed on a stand at a 45 degree angle over a low fire. I was told Father designed it. I am sure we had others helping the cook with the domestic work.

Sitting one evening at the table, some Africans had been out gathering and they brought us some honey combs with lots of bees. Dad made me pick them up, and not show fear. To this day I do not have a problem with bees, even when raiding the hive on the farm with Posto. All we had was some smoke and no protection other than a long sleeve jumper and a scarf around the neck. No hat either. Fear? Through the bees I learnt not to fear people or animals, as Father spoke to me of never showing fear as that creates fear in the animals, but to stay calm. It is the same with bees, as they can smell your fear and it makes them angry.

Later while at Perani a lion came and slept under Father's camp bed. We had a Zanzibar donkey called Michael who was cheeky and bit everyone, except Father. Wherever Dad was, the donkey would find him. One day Michael saw Dad standing near a paw paw tree which had a hive of bees. You can imagine what happened next, the swarm of bees attacked Father.

When we moved to Tanga, I feared the sea and Father towed me out at high tide and left me there to find my way back to shore. Well I love the sea.

Another day we were out walking on the road, when Dad saw a tree frog which turned white when it was picked up. Dad arranged with a worker to take the frog to someone he knew, who would know what to do with it.

Arriving one day from Arusha at Korogwe Station, I saw my poor Mother had had her teeth pulled out, even the good ones. The dentist told her it was his contribution to the war effort. It was here she told me to stand with my legs together otherwise a man would look up my legs. (Education, what?)

We took people with us in lorries, tents and other things, and the car, and went to the sea for Christmas, somewhere near the Kenya border. It was my first Christmas as a family. It was my second time to see the sea. I was given a Bullmouth Helmet (cameo) shell (*Cyraecassis rufa Linne* – East Africa) by the Africans who were with us. A real camping safari. I felt really happy there.

It was then back to the valley again.

Next our home was built from tall grass, where it was, I do not remember the name of the place, but it was here that I met my sister Frederica, born on 7 July 1948 at the Tanga Hospital. Father asked if I would name my sister and I chose Elizabeth after our Royal Princess. I will never forget the look on Mother's shocked face as she said "NO". Father said she had chosen. I have never been forgiven for that choice of name. (Too bad.) I watched Mother feed Frederica with a banana-shaped bottle, known as an Edwardian Glass Baby Bottle.

We had our cats with us, and one day the parents were sitting on the veranda with a bowl of paraffin and tweezers, pulling out the maggots (jiggers). These poor cats had their tummy full of them. Well, the place had red dust. Dad showed me the foundation where they were planning to build a new home; it never happened.

David and Anne Stacey (nee Cecil and Goodrich)

Harry Beer with Mother

Danny Nortje 1955/6

# Makindi by the Sea

Home again, and now we were packing the lorries with our household goods plus the cats in sacks heading for our new home, which was an old Arab house in Makindi, south of Tanga on the Pangani road. We were at the very end of the cliff next to the Mangrove forest, by the sea. At the bottom of the cliff were about three tamarind trees. The property had a few huge mango and coconut trees, also a baobab tree. Mother mentioned the villagers came to claim compensation for the fruit trees, saying they belonged to them. A few of the Africans who worked for Dad, with their families, came with us.

To this day I do not know much about my sister and her baby days. Sometimes Eveline, our nanny, would allow me to push the pram, but often Dad forbid me. Other times I would be in the bedroom with Dad, and it was then I was allowed to be near her, but I don't remember picking her up in my arms.

One thing we gained in our new home were these huge red land crabs who were in residence. Father would feed them with paw paw. Also these people (crabs) would wander around the cliff, but always came home.

I lived in Makindi until I married and moved to the Federation of Nyasaland and Rhodesia in 1960, to live on a farm with Wilfred Haywood.

Fossil and clam shell

## Perani Saw Mill

After arriving in Makindi, building started on sheds and other outer buildings for the timber coming from the Perani Saw Mill. Also the extended buildings to the Arab House, like the kitchen with a store room on one side and on the other side a large sitting room and a side room, where Mother had her odds and ends plus the incubators for the chickens to hatch from the eggs. The added room was an open garage then a large bedroom with veranda.

The bath house had two rooms divided by a passage which was built away from the house. The one room had a cement bath, the same style as the homes in Kulasi. The other room was the toilet. Behind was an open laundry. At the start of our early years, the hot water was boiled in 45 gallon drums on open fire.

Later, part of the land where the baobab stood Father sold to people from town.

Perani Saw Mill was by the Umba River near the Kenya border and some distance from the Indian Ocean, but Perani Hills and a large village, Mwakajembe, were near by. The locals were known for their very good wood carving using ebony, a dark black wood, and sandalwood, a very light type of wood. Both are very hard woods.

Perani by the river was very beautiful. The water was clear; you could see the stone, little fish, or shrimps and water plants. The Africans made long woven-type basket traps from reeds or very thin strips of wood. Up in the trees were the Colobus monkeys (*mbega*; *Colobus guereza*) or away from the river one could see the Vervet monkey (*tumbili*; Clorocebus family: *Cercopithecus pygerythrus*). There were so many birds (maybe you could tell me what they were ...).

Of the many trees I could only recall the sausage tree (*mwgea*; *Kigelia Africana*) with its huge sausage-like fruit as if hanging from a long rope with many flowers hanging from a stem. The flowers are large blood red, maroon in colour. I think they are lovely flowers. When you cut into the seed you get a sap which is used for medicine to treat skin cancer, or ulcers. I am sure there are other uses for the tree.

To start with we lived in tents, while a structure was going up for a one storey home. Father mentioned that one night a lion came and slept under his camp bed. (I felt then that the animal came to guard Father.) As is common when living in the bush, after one's last walk before going to bed you pay your last visit. And this one night Dad got bitten by a snake while walking in the grass. The fang marks only came up a day later, and it was then that Mother arrived with the usual supply for the mill. Soon after paying the people, it was a turnabout for Mum to take Dad to a private hospital in Tanga. He was ill for about six months. Anne Goodriche (previously Cecil) was one of his nurses. Anne later married David Stacey whom she met in Tanga. Dad believed in fresh air, he mentioned that he asked Doctor Zimmerman to move him outside, but the doctor would not allow it.

Massow believed in keeping up the strength of his workers. It was not easy for the staff to go home for lunch. So there were two 45 gallon drums standing on a kind of stand (I do not remember what), but I know there was an open fire, and it was here that the water and maize (*posho*) meal and lots of sugar was mixed. There were two men with a big stick which was used to cook and slowly stir the liquid to make a sloppy porridge (*ugari/ugali*). While I was at Perani with Dad I would go with a bowl to get this lovely porridge for my lunch.

The mill was made up of three huge steam engines to drive the heavy duty vee belts attached to pulleys, which were used to drive the various machinery for sawing logs,

then into plucks to create various widths of timber for different uses. If I remember correctly the steam boilers were acquired from the Amboni Sisal Estate.

The sawed timber was bought to Makindi to be stored ready for sale. The thin planks used for roofing, were kept buried in trenches on the beach to cure them with salt for about three to six months. Father said this would preserve the timber from being destroyed by insects.

The other sideline we had in Perani was a lot of sansevieria cylindrical (straight), a spear shaped plant. This tall rod-like plant grew wild under the trees in a more open area. It produced a very fine silky string. I was there when one of the workers was not quick enough in feeding the cut plants into the decorticator; an accident happened. This poor chap had his hands caught up with the machinery and were chopped off. This type of accident was not common.

There were days when we went for a drive at sunset. Often we would see the various animals, like antelopes jumping over bushes. It is a sight that one does not forget easily.

The residents from Mwambani Village to our end of the cliffs where we lived, wanted electricity in their homes. Up to then lighting was either by generator or pressure Tilly lamps, and Kerosene (paraffin) lamps. They asked Massow to move his factory from the Umba to Makindi. The Electricity Board wanted a factory to make it profitable for them to establish the power line to Mwambani, and the private people who had powerful jobs in Tanga would benefit as their homes would have electricity. It also made it open for more land was sold for private housing.

Timber (logs) was now brought to Makindi, first from Perani. Along this route were many villages, and one could stop by the little *hoteli* to buy food. Father and I would also stop and buy barbequed sticks of meat being cooked over an open charcoal fire. Lovely! On one such stop for the lorries, the driver shouted if all were aboard as there was a blind spot, and the reply was "Yes (*ndiyo*)", but one of the workers instead of jumping in from the back of the lorry used the left side rear wheel just as the driver started to move forward. So you can guess: he was crushed to death. The family was compensated the correct insurance amount. Speaking to Mother about the subject, she mentioned the family came back some time later for more payment.

Once the mill was installed at Makindi, it was easy for me to see the different types of trees used, and the colours of the heart: of the trees when cut. These were dark burgundy red, black or brown like ebony, pinky red. White or pale yellow/white was often the sap part of the wood. Just before I left Tanganyika, Father had found a tree with dark emerald green, but once exposed to light the colour turned darker. I have not been able to find the name of this tree.

On my trip to Oxford, to the Bodleian Library, I found a list of trees growing in the Tanga Provence written up by Forestry Commissions, and I also read books at the British Library from the three East African countries on trees and shrubs. I was pleased to see Swahili names of the trees. From my Oxford list of trees I came across Massow's name and the tree he used for his flooring blocks, *Brochyleana hutchinsii Hutch* (*muhulu*). It was known as sandalwood with a strong perfume, from which oil is extracted, and this is often used in India for funerals. For about two miles down the road you could smell this sandalwood. Dad called this timber "Kalambati" (*Trachonanthis*) which is similar to the *muhulu*, but the crushed sawdust wood was more of a camphor smell. It was a small tree.

To my excitement while I was at the library, I came across Rod Cluers' name and his dealings with Doum Palm (*Hyphaene thebaica*; *mkoma*). The seed is known as white ivory. Father informed me that the elephants helped to germinate the seed by swallowing it and having it pass through their intestines. Dad believed the lack of trees along the coast was due to there being no elephants. The palm leaves were used for basket and mat weaving and plaiting.

My other childish joy, I came across a description of *Erica princeana. Engl*, being one of the plants with Magdalene's name to the plant along with her husband's name Hauptmann Prince s.n, (T) Stolz 2605, from the Utschungwe Mountains, now known as Udzungwa National Park in the lringa District. I had an email from the Berlin Botanical Archives that Granny collected 244 plants from that time in Africa.

Oh! I must not get carried away, so back to Perani Saw Mill.

Massow had one of the steam engine cylinders with all the inner parts, like the pipes, removed. Both ends had doors to close after it was filled with off-cuts from unwanted pieces of wood, then set alight to burn as charcoal. This helped extract the black smokey liquid. I understood from a friend years later, the Americans liked the liquid to give a smoky flavour to foods. But we collected this liquid to treat pools that were to be used in the ground or paint round the buildings to stop the white ants (termites) getting in to eat the timbers, and other things in the house or whatever!

In 1955, just before Frederica and I were due to fly with Mother to Germany to visit her mother, Father was experimenting with a small piece of very hard wood to see how it would turn out planed. The wood shot out and hit his fingers. So he had parts missing and there was Dad in bed, with a bandaged hand, to greet me when I arrived from Kongwa. Lucky for us Danny Nortje was working for Dad. Years later in Rhodesia I met a cousin of his – small world.

We had a contract with Liverpool/Uganda; the company bought our flooring blocks which were exported overseas to England and Italy. Margarete went with the workers to Tanga Harbour when the cargo ship docked, to organise the loading of the blocks. The blocks had to be placed on a huge macrame style net, it was then hoisted by crane and taken into the hold of the ship. There was no time for hanging around. The harbour workers refused to do the loading. It was a time when there could be unrest with the unions.

In 1956 the Suez crisis had started and that was the end of our contract with the Liverpool/Uganda. The transport costs would increase as it meant that all shipping would go round Cape Town, South Africa. Also what would not help, was that Mozambique had better quality *Brochyleana hutchinsii Hutch* (sandal) trees, which they were making railway sleepers from, as the tree grew straight and tall. This lovely wood, with its very line tight grain made it hard for insects to penetrate.

So, again, another change came around for Perani Saw Mill, and different contractors and work. Furniture, building timbers for estate construction, such as doors, roofing, etcetera. Now Dad sought out different trees like mahogany (*Meliaceae*), mvulu (*Milicia excelea*). This majestic very tall tree with its green mulberry type fruit, has the same value as the oak tree of Europe. This tree was used mainly for government furniture and homes. Massow had mvulu planks from his father which were cut before the First World War. Later they were used to make a side board cupboard for Mother. When the family moved to South Africa in 1962, the timber started to crack like my sandalwood furniture I had as a wedding present from my family. Father warned me to design furniture that would have loose panels in the wardrobes due to the dryness of dry inland regions from that of the coast damp areas. Also the sea transport would not help.

Dealing with local companies, one went broke. So Perani lost money, but this company was saved by the Masonic organisation so he could go on working, But? Another contract they had was with a Dutch company who had moved over from Indonesia. Massow informed them that the way they were doing the roofs of the compound housing, the wind would blow them off when there was a tropical storm. They used the same design they used before in Indonesia, as the storms on the Islands were worse than those in Tanganyika. Well the roofs blew off and were then rebuilt to Massow's design.

A!so, the Assam Tea Company moved over to the Eastern Usambara in Amani. Tea was already being grown there.

As Tanganyika Territory politics was slowly changing, people were starting to move out of the country, so furniture was being made and we had an Italian to make the furniture with an Indian, and other workers had to change their way of working. The Italian showed me how to apply French Polish finish on the furniture. It took a few weeks to get this polish up to a high standard of gloss. I must say it was beautiful.

To get the trees for the new work at the mill, Massow had a timber cutting contract with the Ralli Brothers Sisal Estate at Myesani and Lanzoni, in the tropical forests. Then Ah Lain, a Chinese man who had a business interest on the estate, stopped

Dad from cutting the timber. Dad asked for just another year to cut the trees, but Ah Lain said he was going too slow. He wanted the area bulldozed out, to get sisal planted.

Our form of transport for the business were three lorries, the Thames, and Commer, also an army Bedford Truck. This last was used during the heavy rains, as it had a four wheel drive. We also had a short base Land Rover. But the best car to go into the forest for Father was the Volkswagen (Beatle) with its undercarriage being metal sheeting. In the heavy rains, Massow would have a worker go with him, so they could push the car along the ruts made by the lorries. Other than the Bedford Truck the other trucks could get stuck in the heavy wet soil of the forest during the monsoon rains.

I learnt to drive, driving the Land Rover. I also had the help of Ralf Bennet, a friend of Father's from the time they were interned in Southern Africa. He came up from Lindi sometimes to visit us. Anyway I had to help him when he stripped the Bedford Truck engine. It was a good lesson as I learnt how engines worked. Also, it helped me understand how the engine of the Land Rover worked. I found that very useful when I was on the farm in Rhodesia . I often helped women who could not start their cars or change their tyres. The roads were not that safe during our time in Rhodesia when the guerilla war fare intensified.

When the drivers went on strike for two weeks, Dad offered them some other kind of work. The union forbid them to take any other form of work, and if they them found doing other work they would have had their driving license taken from them. They were paid by the unions, but half of what they earned from Father. The Indian then took one lorry to go to the forest to fetch the logs, while I, when I came back from work in town, had to drive the other lorry with the sawdust. This was normal, the dust was returned to the forest and logs brought back. But as only one lorry could be used, I was given the job of taking the other lorry with the sawdust to one of the African Coconut Plantations, where the workers would spread the dust between the trees. As coconut trees do not grow straight, no problem for Father to check how many trees I had scraped with the side of the lorry. Driving along those sandy roads with deep ruts. Well?

Mica mining trench and workers, September 1953

September 1953, background Usambara Mountains, Matai. The little hill - Mbali

Padna June 1953, workers sorting and trimming the mica books to send to Morogoro in boxes.

# Mining

## Mica (phyllosilicate) Mineral

While Father was establishing the sawmill in Perani, he was taken ill after a snake bite. He needed to get better after being six months in hospital. So once out of hospital, Father went to Mlola and opened a mica mine in the Usambara Mountains.

Mica mineral is formed in sheets of silicate (phyllosilicate) minerals in the form of a book (so also known as a book). There are different colours. Ours was brown, while in Morogoro region one could find a dark green which was of a higher grade. Our brown mica was used mainly for electrical insulation, such as in domestic irons. A sheet cut to size was placed between the handle block and the electric heated metal base for insulation purposes.

The mine was situated among hills. On a higher hill the homestead was built, and you could look down on the mine set up of various buildings. One long open building was where the cleaned and sorted mica books were kept. In another shed, the mica was cut by large heavy duty scissors to saleable size, then packed into wooden crates to be taken to Korogwe and transported to Morogoro. The mica was dug out of the ground from long dug trenches following the mica deposit seams.

During my ten-week holiday Mother took us to be with Dad, and the evenings were like magic, when Massow showed us how to identify the various minerals from the stones he had gathered by heating them. I think the green smoke glow could have been copper. What the other colours were, I could not say as it was many years ago and I cannot be sure what method he used.

*A Wondering Man of the Usamabara Mountains & Umba Steppe*

Massow's wonderings helped him get his strength back, and on one of these trips with some workers and using his Geiger apparatus they came across a place where there was uranium, where Father took a piece with him and went straight home to Makindi/Tanga. A Hollander friend introduced him to the Firm Van Eeghen Macclean. These people soon arrived from Holland and off they went with Massow to see if it could be mined. But there was not enough. It was thought a rare find, but they could not identify how it came to be there. I remember Father telling me this and it is in his privately published book, ***Was War Kommt nicht wieder*** (***What was not coming back***).

Massow did a lot of walking in these Usambara Mountains facing the Umba Steppe, towards the Kenya border and down towards Mwakajembe and Perani, then on towards the Indian Ocean. I remember one of these walks to the edge of the mountains and looking towards this huge flat open land to Umba Steppe. Places that he visited were from Songona Mountains, into what is known as the Mkomazi Game Reserve. Then Ugulima eight miles from Ngomazi below the Usambara Mountains. Padna – June 1953. Mabili Upore – September 1953. Perani Great and Small Hills. Also Mponda – Kaitmite, Kupfer, north-west of the Usambaras. These were names written on the back of photos taken during that time. He was always collecting samples of stones, of which he sent 55 to the Geological Survey Department Laboratory in Dodoma. But his most important find was at Gerevi Hills going towards Mwakajembe, where he found a turquoise stone which composition differed considerably from that of accepted turquoise minerals. It attracted the interest of Professor Henry Bassett, Mineralogist Chemist.

I met Professor Bassett during one of my school holidays, when he came to go on safari with Massow. Father took him to Gerevi Hills where he collected his own samples of turquoise. I understand he did a lot of travelling with Father.

There were many stones, but I remember the ruby, mclaya garnet, sapphires, and turquoises. The colours ranged from black, blue, green, red, dark reds, grey to silvery. You name it, it was there for us to stare at in wonder. From a small amethyst stone Dad gave me I had a broach made in the form of a flower, with two small chains with two claws from Mum's fur coat.

Fossils were another thing he brought home for us to see. He gave me a tooth about 2–2½ inch long and about 1½ high with a

Ugulua, 8 miles from Ngomazi on the Usambara Mountains, Ramazani, Tupa, Salim, Samason

Mbalili-lyare, Ramanzi, Asimani, Tupa, Samason

Professor Henry Bassett, minerologist chemist with the diggers

Searching for Minerals
MOSHI
VOI
MOMBASA
TANGA
Lushoto
MOMBO
KOROGWE
1 - Perani
2 - Gerevi Hills
3 - Mlola
4 - Mlalo
5 - Mtai
6 - Mkomazi + Padra?
Plus a few other plac
main roads
2nd roads
Umba river
Border between Kenya/Tanganika

stripy section on the side and on the top was a twisted pattern. Father thought it was from a grass eating animal. He sent samples overseas, but they were not identified. He also had a large slab of rock used as an outside table, with lots of fossils on it, in front of the house in Makindi.

On visits to Mlola at the mica mine, we often went for walks in the bush. On the day we went with Father, Mother, Fidi and Hassani we came to the edge of the mountain, where we looked down and across the Umba Steppe. What an amazing sight, the long distance of flat land.

Well I must have become slightly bored and was playing with a knife when I cut my little left hand finger to the bone. As you can imagine, the bleeding. Well, Hassani found this Jimson weed, took a leaf and squeezed the juice on the finger which stopped the bleeding, then wrapped it with more leaves.

*Thorn Apple – Daura stramonium*: also known as Jimson weed, moon flower, devil's trumpet, plus, and Swahili name *mwiba* apple, muarna.

By the time we came home my finger had turned black, and Father said if there was no improvement the next day we would have to go to town to see a doctor. As luck would have it, my finger was a normal colour with a scar to show where the cut was, which can still be seen to this day. No stitches.

Once I met a young man whose parentage was American, and we were talking about my finger and the weed. He mentioned once the family he was working with in Mexico said that the Mayo people used to drug the maidens before sacrificing them for the Priest's religious practices. Also the Priests would have the plants, but took enough of the drug just for hallucination so they could predict what the outcome of this sacrifice would be. It appears that this plant was used by many people not only for ceremonies, but for medicine.

The plant is prickly, especially the apple, which, when mature has black seeds, but the white trumpet flower with its purple centre is lovely to look at.

Padna, June 1953

Mlola Mica Mine. View above from Mzee Kadiuini Hill

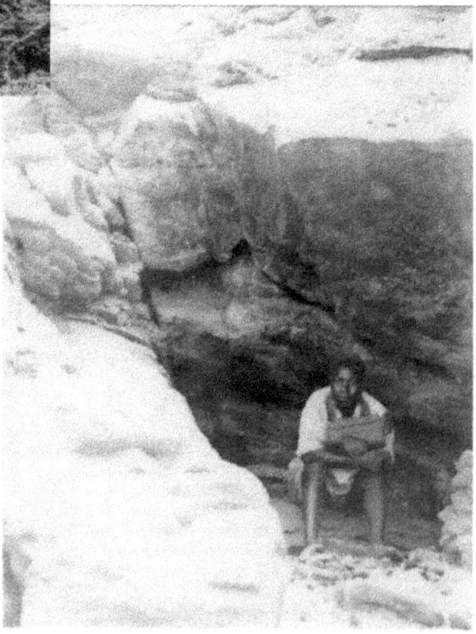

Amisi with the Geigar

# Pakamoyo

Fish Ponds
Shimo la maji
ya Samaki
Pakamoyo
Coconut fronds
used for thatch
Pineapple

Now that we were settled in Makindi, Father was establishing Perani Sawmill, and Mother was organising the coconut plantation and fish ponds, with the occasional visit from Father giving his plans for its future.

Pakamoyo was situated north of Tanga by a river. On a rare occasion Father was talking to me about how he would like to sell the sawmill, and finely develop the coconut plantation and settle here. We were standing below the house where different types of palm trees grew. Massow was already adding to the collection of different kinds of palms.

I must say that Pakamoyo was a lovely peaceful place, with the variety of activity like the various crops being planted, and then with lovely broad leaf grass growing under the coconut trees. Massow said it would be good grassing for cattle.

We had a man who had been in Camp with Father in South Africa in Jagersfontein by the name of Mr GF Braun. He was with us for about a year or so. A very sad person. The workers did not like him, so they played up, like planting the cassava cuttings upside down. Margarete had shown him how to plant the cassava. The cut cassava stick had to be about twenty inches long, of which four inches was put into the ground at a forty-five degree angle. Margarete returned to pay the workers and see what had been done, only to find all the sticks had dried up because the workers had planted the cuttings upside down. I noticed it as I was home from Arusha School at the time. It meant the loss of a crop.

After Father spent six months being ill, the plantation was sold to pay the hospital.

*Coconut Palm – (Coco nucifere)* Member of the Arecaeac palm family

This majestic palm tree, with its many names from various places around the world, decided to make its home in the tropics, whether the sea currents, brought the plant or humans transported the nut while sailing the oceans of this world is not certain Suggestions from fossils found that it could be Australian or Indian 37-55 million years ago. WOW!

Anyway the above name as I know it, is said to come from the Portuguese and Spanish in the 16th century, with COCO meaning grinning face, to grin, make a grimace, or after a witch called Coco, or the brown hairy surface of the coconut, which reminded them of a ghost. But later the name nut was added. But to me, it reminds me of the face of a little monkey like the *tumbili*, also known as *kitumbi*, a small light coloured Vervet monkey.

On the plantation, I watched the harvesting of the nuts. The Africans used to climb the tree with the twisted coir rope done in a rung, which was twisted into a figure of eight and attached to their feet. This helped the person get a better grip of the tree, as they pulled themselves and hopped up the tree. Boy! Could they go up fast, but once at the top they would use their panga (machete) to chop the branch of mature nuts to drop down to the ground.

Once the nuts were gathered, they were taken to where some of the workers stood with an iron rod stuck in the ground. The worker would force or jump the nut into the rod to help open the husk to get the centre where the nut was. Then another worker would use a panga to split the hard nut in half. Then it was laid in the sun to dry the meat (flesh) of the nut. Once dried it was known as copra. When done the copra was gathered and packed into a large hessian sack, stitched up before being sold to a trader in Tanga.

The husks and shells were then burnt and the ash was spread around the trees. I remember Mother being very proud, saying with this method she was able to increase the yield of the trees from 60 nuts when the parents first bought the plantation to an average of 80 nuts per tree the following year.

One not only benefited from the fruit of this lovely tree, like the water from the young nut (*mnazi*, liquid *maji ya madafu*), it was easy to drink by making a hole in the one eye of the nut, You could split the nut and put your figure into the cool soft slimy flesh (lovely to eat), grate the meat fruit, which was then squeezed to get the flesh for cooking, or oil for cooking, or the women would use the oil for their hair and body, or just enjoy eating the meat on its own.

The fronds of leaves were used for weaving or plaiting for various things, such as roofing, mats or making baskets.

The other use of the trees, was to tap the heart of the tree to get it to bleed the liquid to make a type of beer. We would sometimes get a bottle of beer and use it for bread making.

There was a coconut beetle that bore into the heart of the tree. The tree could be infested by the coconut beetle, and if not killed in time, could destroy the tree. Father had a 45 gallon drum with a lot of tobacco leaves. The liquid if poured into the heart of the tree would kill them off. I have often used liquid made from tobacco as a spray when my plants are infested with things like red spider, mealie bug, and other insects that cling to the plant.

A dear friend of the family, Mr Grundy had a workshop in Pangani, making wrought iron goods, teapots and cups from the coconut. He also had a trading boat, taking goods along the coast.

This reminds me of a time a German family were making their way back to Germany from South Africa in an old van-type car. Their son became addicted to the *madafu*, and ended up in bed for a couple of days. He was warned he would be ill if he drank too much of the *madafu*. Once they left I wondered if they made it back to Europe. This was in the 1950s.

*Cassava – Manioc:* (*Manihot utitissina*, an euphorbiacae, sap is poisonous)

Country of origin: Brazil, dating 10,000 years domesticated. After reading Frederich Nartey's book, *Manihot Esculenta – Cassava*, I was really happy that my memory had not left me on this subject.

When we moved to Makindi, five miles south of Tanga, I was nine years old and my sister Frederica was just a baby. I spent a lot of time with the Africans, seeing what they were doing and asking a lot of questions. I would see them gathering food, and cassava was one of the plants. Digging up a potato-like tuber, but not killing the plant off. Also, gathering the young leaves to cook as spinach. Though I did eat some, I do not remember the taste. The Africans explained which cassava I could eat raw, and the other kind that had to be peeled and dried in the sun and would turn black. When dry it would be ground into flour, and later cooked into a kind of thick black porridge like you would do with ground maize.

Swahili: Cassava – *muhogo*, dried tuber – *kopa*, leaves – *kisamvu*, coarse meal – *garri*.

The sweet cassava (*Manihot palmate*) which contained less cyanide compounds, was either eaten raw, or put into hot ashes, or peeled and then boiled. It was okay, but the bitter cassava – (*Manihot untilissima pohl*) manioc, yuco – produced a much higher quantity of cyanide compounds. The Africans would not allow me to eat the bitter cassava, they said I could become ill if eaten raw. Maize did not grow well on the coast, as the soil was too sandy.

*Oyster Nut*: (*Telfaiva pedata* of the Cucurbitacea family);
Swahili – *Mkweme*, *Kweme*
It took me a long time to learn the English name of *kweme* was oyster nut. It is a plant of Africa, mainly East Africa. I read once that the plant grew wild in the Rift valley well north of Nairobi, Kenya.

The long pumpkin-like plant about 50cm long, grows on long thick vines into big trees to support this heavy plant, and fruit, reaching to the top of trees, 30 metres or more. When the fruit turns from dark green to brown it drops to the ground. You then open the pods (if one can call it that) where all the nuts are supported along the length of the fruit. It is very much like cucumber with many seeds.

Gathering the ripe nuts is fascinating, as the hard shell of the nut is wrapped with a woven like casing. Once you cut this fibre covering off, you get to the hard shell. I would bang the side of the nut, and that would split the nut in half. The inside flesh is covered with a grey/green bitter skin. You would then put the nut in hot water, like you would do with almonds to remove the coating.

*Mother's Almond or Oyster Nut cake.*
(You can use other nuts like pecan or macadamia)

½lb ground nuts with the skin. Other than the skin of the oyster nut.

½lb sugar

5 to 7 eggs (depending on the size of eggs)

25 roasted coffee beans ground.

Beat the eggs with sugar until stiff, then add coffee grains and last fold in the ground nuts.

Bake in a prepared cake tin for 3/4 of an hour. (Temp was not mentioned, so I always used a moderated oven}. When cold, half

the cake, (Optional) and add the following filling.
¼lb icing sugar.
6½ oz dark chocolate with a little water, cook to a thick cream.

Stir in 1/4lb butter (which has been creamed) only when the chocolate mixture is cool, you then fill and cover the cake.
To improve the flavour, let it be stored for a day before use.

When I was six years old my maid took me to watch a blood sister ceremony. We were sitting in a horseshoe shape outside one of the huts. Non-members of the family sat a little way. I was invited to sit with the family. These two girls who were to be united, sat next to their mothers. A lot was said, I presume in Kishambaa, the language of the Washambaa people on the estate. Well the girls' wrists were cut from the inside of the arm just behind the wrist. Small strips of the oyster nut (*kwere*) were given and the mothers held the arms of the girls, and then dipped the nut in each girl's blood, then the nut they fed to each opposite girl. Now the mothers took the arms of their daughters and rubbed the blood on their wrists together in a fashion of binding them together.

*Pineapple*: (*Ananas comosus*, Bronmeliaceae family)
Swalihi name – *mnanasi*; *nanasi*

King of Fruit
*There is not a nobler fruit in the universe* (Jacob Bontius, 1628)
*Every fruit has its secrets* (DH Lawrence, 1923)
(From Frau Beauman's book, *The Pineapple – King of Fruits*)

The history of this wonderful fruit starts its journey in the south of Brazil and Paraguay. The Tupi-Guaranus society used the term *anana*, meaning an excellent fruit of fragrance, as well as *nana* referring to the plant as a whole. The Tupi-Guaranus travelled in their long canoes, holding around 30/60 people navigating the rivers and seas of South America and into the West Indies.

I remember once reading a book on how the missionaries took the *ananas* to Hawaii from the West Indies. They had a difficult time establishing the pineapple to grow, until casuarina trees were planted along the coastal belt to filter the sea air. The

Portuguese were responsible for introducing the pineapple along the coast of West and East Africa, while the Dutch East India Company – Jan van Riebeck and the Dutch farmers – established the pineapple at the Botanical Garden, Kirstenbosch, in South Africa, Cape of Good Hope. From there the pineapple spread up the continent of Africa.

The planting of the pineapple on the coconut plantation, just above the cliff on the sandy soil was ideal for the crop. This beautiful plant with its individual little purple/blue flowers on each section as the fruit was developing with its crown of leaves. I never realised that each triangle section of its flower formed multiple fruit, coalesce berries, which all joined up on the one steam that is the middle of the plant.

The *ananas* takes about two years to mature. The plants were planted in rows and always looked untidy with all its long spiny leaves and succulents. Once the fruit is harvested, the top can also be cut off and left to dry a little before planting. But this is not done as the fruit is sold with the top growth of leaves. There are various cultivars, the biggest one I saw at the market was from Zanzibar. All I know was that ours were not as big as the Zanzibar variety.

*Fish Ponds*

I do not know too much about the fish ponds, only they were down the embankment by the tidal creek. The ponds were fed by sea water and fresh water seeping from spring water coming through the cliffs.

The Government Fishery Officer came to talk and advise on the subject, on what type of fish to put into the ponds. My parents often referred to that lovely book: *The Sea Fishes of Southern Africa*, by JLB Smith. Talapia was mentioned, otherwise of the rest I have little knowledge, except the large prawns taken to a man who worked at Davis Ltd in Tanga.

A guard was employed with a gun, as crocodiles had found easy pickings in the ponds.

Father pointed out a large outcrop of gypsum to the left of the ponds jutting out of the cliff.

The clam shell is a fossil that one could find in the high cliffs in Mwambai. The cliffs were old sea beds. Father had two. One he gave to the Pietermartizburg Museum in South Africa

The fishermen always brought their unusual catch of various types of sea creatures, also a hammer head shark to show my parents.

*Tropical Fruits*

I have always been fascinated with plants, how they grow, what can be eaten or not. Their uses are many. So I decided to read and write about the plants I had come across during my time in Tanganyika, roaming around with the natives or on my own as a young girl. What grew where we lived or other people's homes, adding Latin names, as well as the odd Swahili name as I remembered it.

Arusha School always gave us children various fruits in season for our 10 o'clock break.

AVOCADO – (*Persea America*) There are many varieties. The one I enjoyed eating most was a very small one with dark silky skin that grew in Kalange, with sugar. Aunt May had many trees growing outside her kitchen and dining room window. These grew wild in Colombia I was told by a lady I met years later when having treatment in Bircher Benner, Zurich, Switzerland.

BANANA – (*Genica Musa*) Arusha had people making their homes using banana leaves for roofing. These Warusha lived among the groves of very tall banana plants on the slopes of Kilimanjaro and Meru. I was told there were at least 25 different kinds. I remember seeing the fat red skinned banana, or fat green ones which were only used for cooking or placing them with the skin in hot ashes to cook. Then there was the Lady's Finger. It was small and sweet.

We had a visit of a family from Voi on holiday, as Mother had a Bed and Breakfast. These people had come to the seaside. Anyway, she mentioned there was one banana she could dry, and then be able to make her bread. She would not give me her recipe, but I gave her my special shortbread cake. Mum always made me make it when people came. Oh well!!

CACTUS / Prickly Pear – (*Opuntia speci.*) Mother made a jelly from the fruit when we were living in Kulasi. As there was no fridge, the jelly was put into a dish and put outside at night in a very cool place for it to set.

CAPE GOOSEBERRY – (*Physalis peruviana*). We only boiled the fruit for desserts or just picked them from the bush and ate them like that. Birds really loved them too, so the seeds got spread out in the bush.

CASHEW TREE – (*Anacardium occidentale*) The tree produced a fruit (apple) when ripe red, which we did not eat, but the nut in its hard casing developed outside of this apple. It is an evergreen tree. I heard some people made a drink from the fruit.

CITRUS – So many kinds of fruits and varieties, from oranges, naartjies (tangerines), grapefruit (we had the white flesh variety), lime and lemons. The kind I liked had a soft skin, and you could eat both the peel and the fruit. At Arusha we girls would peel the orange carefully as not to break the skin, when done, we would throw the peel over our shoulder to see what shape the skin has fallen, was it a C for Charlie, or S for Sam, etcetera. Always looking for boys' names.

COCONUT – (*Coco nucifera*) The young nut water was lovely to drink on a hot day, also to eat the flesh. The African ladies with their thick longish hair, used to plait it in two to four/six rows all along from the front to the back. When they tried to do my hair, I was told it was no good, it just would not keep. They used oil from the coconut.

CUSTARD APPLE – (*Annona muricata* or *reliculate*) I know of three kinds. The one with the rough bubbly shin was more available, while you could find the large kind, green or dark pinkie shine with a smoother skin.

DATES – (*Phoenix dactylifera*) When the dhows in February arrived just before the monsoon rains from Arabia, bringing with them lovely things like carpets, and dry shark meat. But best were the dates stored in large baskets. When the Royal Navy called at Tanga after a time checking the boats up north, they would tell us stories, like how dirty the dhows were and the huge cockroaches all over the place.

FIGS – (*Ficus Sur*) The wild fig growing across sub-Sahara to South Africa. This kind was the one we could eat, but had to be careful there were no worms or other insects in the fruit. I remember a big tree grew in the Arusha School grounds. There was one growing by the river between Kulasi and Magoma, as I went there often with Chambo and other African children to play in the river. We were told not to go to the tree at night, for it was the time when the Devil (*Shetani*) came out to start his night roaming. I was also told that people looking for gold in Africa took the dried fruit with them. This is how the seeds would spread and grow across Africa. The birds love the fruit.

FIGS – (*Ficus Carica*) European type of fig grown by people in their gardens, which is where I came across this type of fig. I must say the inside looked similar to the wild kind, but was more spongy in texture.

GUAVA – (*Psiduim guajava*) We had the white guava growing in the gardens. We would stew them as well as eat them raw. I never remembered making jam. The birds loved them too, the seed dropping spread the growth of trees in the bush.

INDIAN ALMOND – (*Terminalia catappa*) These beautiful majestic trees with their horizontal branches grew by my office while I was working for Lehmans Limited, a hardware store, in Tanga (Head Office was in London). The broad leaves would turn from green to various shades of copper, from light to mahogany colour. The fruit could be eaten when the fruit turned from green to dark purple. But I never managed to crack the nut.

JACK FRUIT – (*Artocarpus heterophy*) Swahili: *Fenesi*. The huge khaki green coloured fruit could weigh from 10–20 pounds, but has been known to weigh up to 100 pounds. When ripe, there are a lot of segments of a shiny yellow, but smelling like over-ripe peaches. Many people are put off by the smell. I enjoyed eating them.

LITCHI / LYCHEE – (*Litchi chinensis*) We could buy the fruit at the Sunday market in Tanga. I have never again seen the lychee so big as we had from Zanzibar.

LOQUAT – (*Eriobotrya japonica*) I came across this sweet sour yellow fruit with a large pip in Lushoto. I like sour fruits.

MANGO – (*Mangifere inica*) So many kinds, from large to very small, round or kidney shape with large seeds. Other than the seeds one could eat the whole fruit. Delicious! In the old variety the seeds used to be hairy and threads would get stuck in between the teeth. We did not mind, as we would wash the seed then pretended we had a powder puff.

Mother used to cook the half ripe mangos like one would cook an apple for apple sauce.Apples were expensive on the coast as they was grown in the highlands (transport costs!) Then she would grate raw potato, set aside the potato to turn a little black. When ready she would take a spoon of the grated potato and fry it in deep fat, like you would do chips. It really tasted good with the mango sauce. I must point out our African cook (*mpishi*) Hassani did the cooking. Mother only got her confidence once Father passed away in 1987. She mad a lovely sponge cake.

MULBERRY TREE – (*Movus*) We had the black kind of mulberry tree, The fruit we either had stewed or ate raw, even with added cream. I had a book on wine making, so at the age of 19, I thought I would try my luck in a primitive way on the coast. There was a semi-dark cool place in Mother's kitchen, where the temperature seemed to stay the same all year round. So I took the clay crock that had been used for pickling or making sauerkraut. Father mentioned when I was not there, that the family had it for Christmas two years later and it was good.

# Schools

One hears how schools were started in new colonial countries depending which colony one lived in. Where I lived it was first known as German East Africa, and after World War One the country became Tanganyika Territory. Schools that one came across at first were German, Greek, Swahili, Missionary, Government as well as Private, then English. But before the territory was divided into the various countries the Church Mission Society had their Headquarters in Mpapwa, which was more central in Tanganyika. Pastor Paul Ansorge, my great-great-great Grandfather belonged to this mission society. His posting was first in Bengal, India. Here his three children were born, and in 1858 he was transferred to Mauritius, before retiring in Liegnizt, Silesia, Germany now Poland, where he settled with his orphaned grandchildren May and Tom Prince. His son Dr William John Ansorge when working as a doctor in Uganda in Kampala, applied to work with the Mission Society in Mpapwa but was declined.

From a trip to The National Archives in Kew I came across how my three schools that I attended in Tanganyika come to be built and why in the places they were located (see map on p8).

## Lushoto School

Lushoto School was first known as the ***Deutsche Schulverein fur den Nord*** (The German School Association/Society for the North). It was in existence in 1930. The school buildings and grounds comprised three areas approximately 15 acres owned by different people. It later became known as Public Ground under a Trustee School founded in 1935. On 3 September 1939 custodianship was administered successively by a Mrs Fraser and by Mr Smith, the then tenant of the school who had the right to occupy the land for education, and was running the school as Headmaster. Mr Smith was my first Headmaster.

When 1 was six years old I went as a border for one year in 1945. Mother took me to the bedroom, and from there one could look down onto the road and across to the river from a high window of what was then the dormitory. Looking down the wall to the road, I saw my mother walking away at the bottom on the road. The school was built on a hill. I was alone. I do not know what happened next. In fact my time in Lushoto was confusing. I do not remember a classroom, dining room or anything. In the dormitory I remembered my bed and where I kept my little family. I went to school with my six tortoises, which I kept in a large basket with grass as bedding by my bed. After school, I would take the little ones to graze in the grass at the back of the dormitories, until one day one of them disappeared. I gathered the others up into the basket, and started to look for the missing one, until the matron told me to leave the others out, and I would find them in the morning. It never happened. I met Mr Smith again when he came to visit my parents in Tanga, and he informed me that the tortoises were still in the grounds of the school. That was 1958/59.

Mother gave me some lovely books with beautiful old fashioned water colour paintings in the Edwardian/Victorian style. In a short time they were gone. I remembered reporting the matter to an adult person. I never got them back, but still remember the beauty of the pictures. A good introduction of how things can happen and knowing you are on your own.

What I enjoyed at that school was that at the bottom of the hill was a brook and one could have little gardens. I had such a garden and after school would work on the plot. I still enjoy working with plants. By this river was a flat piece of ground used for sport. Behind the school was a path leading into the forest behind the school. It was here I saw a ladybird insect, when an elder child told me the rhyme: "Ladybird, Ladybird fly away home, your house is on fire, all except Ann, as she is under the frying pan."

Later years when working in Tanga, if a tourist ship called to Tanga, which was seldom, people could go in a bus/coach to Lushoto to see this colourful market with the women wrapped in their beautiful cloths, with one used as head covering and down the back. The women also rolled colourful tissue paper and used to decorate down the side of theirs ears. Lushoto Town was beautiful.

## Arusha School

The primary school for European children was built by the government in the 1930s, but opened in 1934 to take in pupils as boarders; under the Association of the Bishop of the Anglican Diocese of Central Tanganyika and the Church Missionary Society of Kongwa and Mpapwa. The school's responsibility and administration under the Bishop's wardenship lasted for 18 years.

Though the agreement was from 1933 to 1963 between the government and the Diocese of Central Tanganyika, the terms were that the government agreed to build and equip the school, and maintain the buildings and grounds, employ staff and pay their salary.

The first Headmaster was Reverend William Wynn-Jones (1934-1945), with his wife come from Kongwa, with Miss Martha Vance Missionary Nurse from Mpapwa and his two large tortoises. During my time, there was only one who lived mainly by the avocado trees, and near the sports fields. We often would polish him with boot polish.

During this time Rev. Wynn-Jones had the swimming pool built with a large concrete diving block and a spring board. This was surrounded by a very large fir tree hedge. The playing fields were surrounded by rows of trees, such as large avocado trees growing near the girls' block of dormitories. The far side were the pepper trees (*Schin's moiie*). The various sports we had were cricket, hockey, netball, rounders, football, physical training, and athletics.

Education: Rev. Wynn-Jones introduced Swahili lessons. The children sat Cambridge Junior and Preliminary examinations (these was later cancelled). After these exams children either went to Kenya or elsewhere for higher education.

Government took over the management of the school after Rev. William Wynn-Jones retired in 1946 and the appointment of the second Headmaster Mr Cyril Hamshere (1946-1964), who

Main school building facing Mount Meru. Behind the right hand arch was the Headmaster's office. Behind this double building is the large Hall and the kitchenes throguh that.

Side wings of the main building were the classrooms.

Double storey building - girls' dormitories. Left side of the door were the staff rooms. Right hand side the dormitories. Behind as you walk in were the bath rooms. Stairs were on both ends of the dormitories.

New buildings for the juniors. You walk into the main big hall. It was in this hall we heard of the death of King George. Right hand side, junior dormitories. Left hand side, kitchens and sick bay.

was the son of an Archdeacon JE Hamshere, who had been Principal of the Diocesan Training College for pastors and teachers. Though the school was no longer under the wardenship of the Bishops, it still had its own Chaplain. In my time it was Rev. JD Casson who retired in 1952. Teachers and staff were Government Officers recruited through the Crown Agents in London. We were told that staff had to learn Swahili as well and sit the exams. Africans worked as domestic staff, kitchen staff and ground staff.

The old German School in Oldeani was reopened as a temporary branch school in 1950 and remained open for only two years.

There were always additional buildings being built as there was an increase of pupils from different nationalities, like the German and Greek communities who joined the British children.

The main building had two quadrangles on either side of the hall/dining room, kitchen and office. Also the Headmaster's office was near the entrance to the school. On the left side of the dining room were the boy's domitories, as well as the classrooms, which could be seen from the front of the buildings. On the right side near the kitchen, which was behind the dining room was the sick bay, where I spent time with yellow jaundice and endless nightmares of huge red/brown rolling rocks coming towards me until I fell off into a hole. The rest of the rooms I do not remember what their uses were.

Just outside, at the back of the kitchen was a huge cooling house made from wire and charcoal walls, with water dripping down the walls. Also ferns were growing on the outside. The inside had a concrete floor. I could sometimes see big bowls of jelly if the door was open, plus other foods.

On the right side of the building was a long open corridor leading to the girl's dormitory. Next to this passage was a huge wild fig tree where we would eat the fruit sometimes. Not sure if it was the *Ficus sur* or *Ficus sycomorus*. This building was double storey.

A new building was built for the younger children, which had a new sick sanatorium, its own kitchens, dormitories, classrooms and very large hall with a stage. It was here we heard of the death of King George VI in 1952.

Driving into the school on the left side, first was the Headmaster's house and other homes for the staff. There was a river on the left of the buildings. Going down to the river were a lot of lemon trees. Other staff had rooms in the main buildings, like the matrons who were placed in the buildings near the children. On the way down was a bridge over the river which one could walk across to the Anglican Church. Further down the river was the railway bridge.

I do not remember all the teachers, but here are a few. One could not forget Mr Hamshire, as I was often brought to his office on a Saturday to face him and the prefects to be disciplined for something I had done wrong. I do remember being punished for pinching lemons. One of the prefects reported me, yet they also ate the lemons. Mr Hamshere asked if I enjoyed eating lemons, and my reply was, "Yes". So I was given 100 lines to write. Two weeks later l still had not written them, so l was told to bring my desk on Sunday and place it in front of the master's office, and the lines were now increased to 1,000 lines. So I missed the Sunday walk.

Rev. DT Casson, 1949-1952. I remember he told me that it was time I was christened, which to this day I am not. I did not like the way the priest was preaching in the church on Sunday.

Miss E Latimer, Bursar and part time teacher, but she was first with the Church Mission Society, 1943-1964.

Mrs EM Fisher, Senior Matron 1950-1959. Often she invited me to her home for tea. When I was in Arusha in 1960 I went and visited her again.

Mrs Forrest. My matron in the girls' dormitory 1949-1950. The other matron I do not remember. Yet one of these ladies had a Pekingese dog, which l sometimes would take for a walk in the garden. But this dog had a habit, it would attack you so you made a fast run down the stairs until you were outside, then all was well.

Mrs MH Frost, who taught English, also swimming and guides. And Miss ME Taylor, music teacher. She introduced Carols by Candle Light. Miss Taylor taught me how to play the piano. She had a beautiful Rhodesian Ridgeback dog. Both these teachers were transferred to Kongwa.

Mount Meru, the daily view from the school

*Arusha – on the foot hills of Mount Meru*

A town I stayed in during my school days from 1946 to 1951. Though my fellow students and I spent our time in the school grounds, except when we went home for the school holidays, we were made aware of the interesting things happening around us. So more hotels were built due to the influx of safaris to places like the Serengeti, Ngorongoro Crater, and Lake Manyara, surrounded by flat plains and hills. Filming companies came mainly from America, also big game hunters.

The New Arusha Hotel was established in 1894 (German East Africa) at the time of horse and buggies and classic cars. The roads were another story. They were not paved in tar, but muddy and rutted roads, made worse during the rainy season, which did not help. Can you imagine the ladies with their long dresses and coats? How times have changed!

During my time, The New Arusha Hotel building design had not changed that much (looking at old photographs). But, what little I remember, from when I stayed with my mother when she visited me, was a ceramic black cat with a long tail and rows of doughnuts placed through the tail.

The New Safari Hotel was established in 1935. After I left Arusha more hotels were built and the Conference Centre, with the increase in trade and the increase of visitors from around the world.

**Arusha School - I am standing behind Mr Cyril Hamshere.**
**Have you spotted Miss Taylor's Rhodesian Ridgeback?**

What I think was unique at The New Arusha Hotel, was a sign on a board declaring the exact spot marking the halfway point between Cape Town (South Africa) and Cairo (Egypt). But that was not enough, it was the centre point where the three territories marked the meeting point of Kenya, Uganda, and Tanganyika Territory (Tanzania).

*The Great North Road* coming from South Africa through Southern Rhodesia (Zimbabwe), Northern Rhodesia (Zambia). (Also, once known as the Federation of Rhodesia and Nyasaland or Malawi). Some of the towns saw huge transport lorries come through Beit Bridge (Border Post), onto Bulawayo, Gwelo (Gwero), Salisbury (Haran), Karoi, Chirundu, a border post or from Bulawayo to Victoria Falls and Livingstone on ther way to Lusaka (Border Post), then on to Lusaka. Mpika, up to Tunduma (Border Post}, through to Mbeya, lringa, Dodoma (centre point for Tanganyika Territory), past Konda, where there are old bushmen rock paintings. Then arriving in Arusha, before going on to Longido and Namanga (Border Post), finally heading for Nairobi, Kenya. During this long drive one must remember the roads were often heavy red mud during the rainy season, so it made it hard to prevent getting stuck or avoiding tipping the lorries on their side. Not easy driving.

On our shopping days, we could go to the stores for purchases; always a teacher with us.

One day we were taken to the cinema to watch the film *Black Beauty*. A very sad film which left a lot of us girls crying. It gave the boys a chance to tease us girls.

Sunday afternoon, after tea, was walk time, either going to the railway bridge following the river that flowed along the school boundary, or walking through town, in crocodile form, or should I say "Two by Two"? Being bored, we started to learn how to whistle with our fingers. In later years I found this knowledge very useful; instead of shouting to draw the attention of my family when they were on the far side of the road just whistle with your fingers.

While walking up the stairs from the platform at Paddington Station in London a Supervisor was trying to get the attention of a worker with no hard hat on, and using a jack hammer. I said to him he should whistle. The reply was he could not whistle, so no problem to me, my little fingers went into my mouth and out came a very sharp shrill sound, which the worker heard, plus a lot of passengers who stopped to see what was happening. Boarder school training, what?

*Education*

After a year in Lushoto Schools, at the age of seven years I went to Arusha School and started there until I was twelve, and then went on to high school in Kongwa.

I really do not remember what I thought of my lessons, or the teachers. But when I was nine I seemed to have had a problem, like spelling – e.g. enuf instead of enough. I can still hear the male teacher trying to drum it into me, I was sitting at the back of the class. Then in the Swahili lessons we were taught we would have to join a word or two together, but I just joined the whole lot together with no spacing, just like a long train. Needless to say I got into trouble. Ha, Ha.

Sewing classes I enjoyed, as I seem to have remembered what I learnt. We first had to saw a sewing apron, to put our work in the bag that was part of an apron. We learnt bead work, embroidery. How to sew a shirt by hand, before we were taught how to use the hand-winding sewing machine. We also had to cut cardboard in a circle, with wedges on it, which we used for weaving. The small handbag I made, Mother gave it to a friend as a Christmas present. That knowledge I still have to this day. I also made a bead sailing picture like a tapestry, which I got back from Mother when she passed away.

One time Mother arranged for a lady, who came from Moshi, to give me extra lessons in English. I had to learn poetry and recite it to her. But this did not last long. I wonder why? During my holidays Mum tried to give me extra lessons, but it was easy to run away into the mangrove trees or walk over the sea and the corals, when the tide was away.

The product work we did when I was eleven went to the Police Station.

Here we learnt how to use plaster of Paris, to get the foot or tyre impressions for evidence. We walked around the Station. We then went to the Colonial Insecticide Research Unit, where we saw the breeding of the mosquito. Seeing these wiggling larvae in a tank of water, I do not remember what was said, but have read that the female needs to eat blood for her egg development. We know that where there is a lot of water in a warm climate it is a good breeding area for mosquitoes, like it was on the sisal estate.

After these trips to the Police Station and Research Unit, when we got back to school we had to write about what we had learnt, also draw a map of where we had been in relation to the school.

Oh, I must just mention in our last term before leaving to go to High School, the girls were called to the Headmaster's home and had a talk and support with illustration on the reproductive system of humans. The Headmaster's wife spoke with us girls. Also she showed us how to change an electric plug. The boys went to the Headmaster. When these talks were finished, we children avoided looking at each other.

Part of us from the same class at the police station. Mother never believed in school unifroms. I had a brown hat and not a grey one. Our dresses were bottle green.

*Music: School Choir, Plays*

Our music teacher was Miss Taylor who always appeared to love many children in the choir. It did not matter if you could sing or not. It was more the merrier, and I felt it was a joy to be part of all this singing. Miss Taylor was a few years later transferred to Kongwa. Our new music teacher insisted that we had to be auditioned. It did not matter if you had been part of the choir or not for a few years. I was too nervous to sing on my own, so never made it. Funny I can see her face as I write this. She had black hair and a hard face. Once Miss Taylor left, this woman was my piano teacher, and there I did not last long either. I always had my knuckles smacked with a ruler.

Miss Taylor suggested that I took up with violin. I said no, but had to wait another year before I could have piano lessons, which in later years I realised had been a mistake,

There were various school plays, also folk dancing, but I never joined. But in the first years we had May Pole dancing and I took part in that one year.

We had a percussion band, where we were taught to use the various instruments. Mine was usually the drum with two sticks. (I think it is called a snare drum, or just rat-tat rat-tat). But that did not last.

My first year in Arusha, I was seven years old, we had a young teacher, Miss Silvia Kaufman. She must have been 13/14 years old. Being the war years, there was a shortage of teachers. Miss Kaufman often invited us to her room to hear her play the guitar. She later trained as an opera singer.

One year there was a bad case of polio, and we had our lessons under the trees. But there was one boy who had polio very badly and he was put into an iron lung. When he recovered and was back at school, his father made him have piano lessons to get his fingers to move again. Poor chap he often cried in pain.

When in standard two Rev. Casson asked us to sing a little song in the class. I told the teacher I did not know any but was amazed when I mentioned I could only sing a German song, and that was *Schiaf mein Kindchin, Schlaf ein* (Sleep my child, fall asleep). It is a famous lullaby. Mother had an old fashioned winding gramophone, on which I used to play her records. I often felt isolated and a little frightened at school, Amazing as I started to write, memory flashed in my mind and all the old feelings came, and I felt my mother nearby.

*Dining Room Hall*

This amazing room was huge, so much happened there, not just eating, but entertainment.

When entering the hall from the entrance there were glass cabinets with all sorts of interesting things displayed in them. Then you saw the long dining tables, and benches with a chair at the end of the table for members of staff. I do not remember how many there were. As you look to the wall at the end of the hall, there was a huge oil painting that seemed to fill the whole wall.

The subject was the country showing Mount Kilimanjaro and Mount Meru. One year someone threw a lump of butter which left a stain on the picture.

To the left of this picture was a door leading to the kitchen, which led to other parts of the back of the building. On the right side there was the sanatorium. I remember it well. A dark room. The kitchen porters' place, where I watched the Africans wash the plates, pots and pans by hand. To this day I can still see the back of the diner plates were greasy. All the staff were black Africans, except the lady housekeeper who was in charge.

Behind the kitchen, outside, was the coal-like building, which was built in a frame with coal which was held by wire mesh. There was always water dripping down with ferns growing on the outside. This old style of cool room is where our fresh food was kept, like milk, butter, and jellies when made, whatever other foods that had to be kept cool. I was always looking around the place, and one day the door was open, so I had a good look inside.

Every Sunday half the dining room had ice cream, and the other half had jelly. I never liked ice cream, until one day, when I was nine years old the teacher was fed up, with me and made me eat the ice cream. (Mother always had ice cream at the Korogwe Hotel, she could never understand why I would not have any. I still see her face full of enjoyment when she ate it.)

The other food we did not like was the dark unappetizing spinach, and when the teacher was not looking this delightful mess would find its way under the table, until the House Keeper realised we had to eat our SPINACH, so cheese was added to this delightful ingredient. I must say I still add cheese, as I did for my family. Mid-morning break we mainly had fruit of one kind or other. Oranges were fun, because we would try to peel the skin as one piece. This coil we would through over our shoulder to see how it would land and form a letter, like a C, G, J or whatever. Then we girls would think who was the boy's name, like Charlie, John or whatever took our fancy. (Amazing at that tender age, us girls were thinking of our future role of being married and having children. Is that nature's way of preparing us for motherhood?)

Other fruits were passion fruit (*Passiflora ligularis*), the big yellow/orange fruit, which we called "Snot Nose" on account of its grey/cream flesh colour. Mangos, in those days were lovely and juicy, with hairy flesh. We had bananas.

*Entertainment*

The tables and benches were pushed against the wall, and we had often to sit on the floor. Chairs for the adults.

One time I remembered a man came with his pet chimpanzees. He had arranged tables and chairs and tea things for the chimps' tea party. They were dressed in human clothes, and one must not forget the nappies which were held in place with trousers for the boy, and pretty pants for the girls under their dress. The chimps showed us other tricks too.

Another time people from the Polish Internment Camp in Tengeru, near Arusha, came to perform for us the opera of *Madam Butterfly*. Oh the colours of the cloths, and the floating fine cloth was just out of this world for a small mind like I had then. To think years later here in Aldi, Yiewsley, England, I met a charming Polish lady and her husband. This lady remembers the performance of this play at my school.

Some Saturdays we had dancing. One side of the hall the boys would sit and the girls on the other side. I remember how shy we were with each other. Few boys danced with us girls, so we girls danced the ballroom dance together. I expect we had films too. How the mind runs away from you.

*Girls Dormitories*

As I remembered it, it was a double storey building. The entrance was from the gardens, and the open passage coming from the central block of buildings on the left; there were two steps or perhaps it was one, to enter through the glass door into the hallway. It was here that matron would stand as we filed out to go to breakfast . If matron felt something was wrong she would pull you aside, as she did with me. She told me that my eyes were yellow and sent me off to the sanatorium as I had jaundice. (One girl coming from the gardens tripped on the step and flew into the glass door, and broke it. The poor girl's arms were all cut up.)

To the left, facing the back of the building were the bathrooms. Here was where Sylvia Kaufman had her room. There was a shortage of teachers in 1946 when Miss Kaufman was teaching the seven year olds. Also the left side of the building on both floors were the rooms for Matron and other staff. To the right of both ends were stairs leading to the dormitories. Also on the left side upstairs Matron had her flat.

I have no idea where the laundry was, but we all had a laundry bag for our dirty clothes. It was where we hid our avocados to ripen.

In our bathroom was a locker room before you went to the bathroom itself. The lockers were a small open box like wall. Here we kept our toiletries. Well it was thought that the cleaners must have used our combs, as eight of us girls picked up lice. We were put into a dorm near the Matron's rooms. We were not allowed to mix with the other girls. Only when other students were in class, were we allowed outside to roam the gardens. Poor Matron cut our hair short and washed the hair with paraffin. Our food was brought to us by the kitchen staff, who left the trays on the floor by our door, and when we were finished eating we had to leave the trays outside of the door. Typical of children we enjoyed our freedom.

Telephone training. We were all gathered to learn how to use the hand-winding phone to ring the operator, which, here was to the office, with Matron's help. This phone was outside Matron's private rooms. When it came to my turn, I just had one look at it and fled down the stairs and out of the building. It took me years to overcome the fear of telephoning. But I had no problem setting up a telephone system with two tins and a long string attached to a piece of stick, where there was a little hole to thread the string through. So after lights out we could talk to each other in the other dorms. We would thread the string out of the window then into the next dorm. Or just kept it in our dorm. This happened after lights out, and we could then talk with each other.

*Sports*

I remember being taught how to swim with other children in the shallow end of the pool. Then it was diving, first on the edge of the pool, then the springboard and last on top of the ten-foot concrete block. One day when I was standing on the springboard the teacher told me to pull my tummy in. Well I did not understand what she meant. Another time I dived from the ten-foot board and I landed on my head at the bottom of the pool, and it seemed a while before I came up. To this day I still have that vision of the incident, and I have never been able to dive from that height.

Once a week we had physical training in the morning after breakfast. Some of the equipment we used, like the horse with its adjustable heights. I was never good at jumping over the box. There was balancing on bars, also leap frog. But most afternoons we had sport of one kind or other.

One of the first games I learnt was cricket, when I was seven years old. The usual athletics: I was not good at the sprints, long and high jumps. I enjoyed the archery, I expect because it was one of the games I played with the local Africans in Kulasi. I do not remember much about the other sports.

On one side of the fields there was a wall where we could sit, near the path leading to the main building. It was here that a Catholic Father would come to talk with us during sport sessions. This was a joy to us who had no parents to visit us at school. I was told the Anglican Priest has a family.

I cannot help, but I must mention this: When I had my family, and was watching Anita play rounders, I heard the teacher say, I do not know who that girl is, but she has no ball sense. Their father was really good at cricket. So when I got home I said to Wilfred that we had to play cricket to help the children play cricket. Something I remembered from my Arusha days.

*Half Term – Picnics*

Being boarders and not going home for those Half Term days, the school arranged picnics. Going out into the country at such

School picnic. Parents took some of us on a picnic by a river. Names forgotten

times, we once went to a forest with a hilly slope. We were taught how to run down a steep hill. Never go straight but zigzag your way down the hill. Going down straight you can pick up speed, and one can end up landing flat on your nose. I know, as I am not very good at listening, I often wanted to do things my way. There was the freedom of exploring.

Open lorries arrived at the school, and the dining room benches were placed in the lorries for our sitting. One of the vehicles had the school staff to make the tea on open fire to boil water in a large milk can with a tap. We had picnic-type food, like sausage roils.

We had been to this forest before. On one of these trips, we had a lot of rain on our way back to school and got soaked to the skin. So when we got to school, Matron was having a hard time to get our hair dry, and hot baths. As the years went by, I realised that when washing my hair, I did not have to dry it as I never got that cold we were always threatened with. To this day, I do not dry my hair when it is washed.

What I enjoyed was the singing on our way home or to the picnic site. Songs like "Ten green bottles hanging on the wall". Others – "One man went to mow, went to mow a meadow with his dog", counting up to Ten Men. So we also sang it in Swahili: *Mtu moja ana humba lima shamba na umbwa yake, Watu mibili wana hamba lima shamba na umbwa yake*, and so forth until you reached ten. Then this one tells the story of poor people:

*Moja, mbili, tatu. Mama ana kula viatu. Mtoto ana lia. Baba ana kimbia. Moja, mbili, tatu.* (One, two, three, mother eats a shoe, child cries, father runs away, one, two, three.)

There were lots more songs of the time, like: "You are my Sun Shine".

One time Mother came on a visit and we stayed at The New Arusha Hotel, which was near the school. Other times I went with friends and their parents for the day. But one I remember most was with Prince Isenberg and his family on their farm. They had a wigwam in the garden and making fudge. What a treat. Also, eating raw turnips. Cannot say I am fond of them today.

*Brownies and Girl Guides*
*Motto – Be Prepared*

Being a Girl Guide taught me a lot and what I really enjoyed was

The whole Guide Group

Me sitting in the front with no hat and I see a few faces of girls who went to Kongwa.

Group of us in the school truck going to the Moshi swimming pool. We stayed in Moshi for a week at the Anglican Rectory.

At the Octangle (8 corners octagon) pool. Massowia had no swimming costume. Miss Frost, our Guide Leader.

Moshi Market.
We saw the Chagga carrying their money in coins to the bank.

being with this group of people both at Arusha and Kongwa Schools. Our group leader was Miss M Frost.

We had outings in Arusha, like a trip we did to Moshi and stayed at the Rectory residence. We travelled in the school's open back Ford truck. Once there, we were taken to see other places. Such as a couple of times swimming in the octagon-shaped town pool. Boy! was the water cold – it came direct from the snows of Kilimanjaro, another mountain that dominated a town by its height (Kibo, 5,895m, 19,340ft. is the highest point of the three volcanoes. Mawenzi, 5,149m and Shiru. 3,962m).

We went to shop in the Moshi Market. Interesting walking about, until we noticed the Chaggas (a local tribe) coming with big money bags full of shilling coins, being payment for selling coffee beans from their farms. The Chaggas did not trust the paper money.

I am grateful to have been for so long a Guide. The things you had to learn to get badges. We did map reading with the compass, Morse and semaphore. At that time we learnt to do the alphabet with our hands, The five fingers were the vowels A E I O U. Useful to spell out for deaf people. How to make a camp fire with a square layout of sticks and wood on top of each other. We would sit around it and sing songs like, "Red Men Tall and Quaint with Feathers on our Head", "Alouette gentile Alouette", "*Frere Jacques*", "Ging gang goolie-goolie", (this is a Polonaise lullaby song. I used to sing that to my babies. My son's wife in Australia was surprised I knew the song. Then we had a lot of English songs like "London's burning", "Underneath the Spreading Chest-nut Tree", "There's a hole in my bucket". It really shows how international this movement is, including the Cubs and Boy Scouts. Lord Robert Baden-Powell and his family started the movement after his military time in South Africa.

We learnt to cook potatoes in the hot ashes, or meat on sticks over hot coal. But what amazed us, was making a bag from grease-proof paper. You add water into the made bag, then you can poach an egg, or other thing, s. This was placed on the fire that had died down but still had the right heat.

First Aid was interesting. It taught us how to use our triangle scarf, which was folded in such a way that we used it as a tie, but we could unfold to use as a bandage, sling and other things. Also

I did Life Saving in Kongwa. All I learnt in these lessons, I used when I was married to a Rhodesian farmer, treating our African labourers and their families. I understood how to treat the staff and my family. Our headman on the farm had an abscess on his leg, and the medicine from the hospital did not heal. So we washed it with warm salty water and then added M&B powder on the wound and left it open to dry with air.

Our uniform was blue. I belonged to the kingfishers, and had the colours sewn onto my shoulder. Also our whistle in a looped lance line was wound around under our arms.

*Extra Trips – between 1947 & 1952*

In what year? I just shrug my shoulder. Trips organised by the Headmaster and staff. I enjoyed getting out and seeing something different.

*Farm – Wild Animals*

The animal farm was north of Arusha on the road towards Kenya. The farm organised the capture, and collection, of live wild animals to ship to the world zoos. While we were there a high caged lorry with animals came to be penned in fenced *bomas.* This game farm we visited too, was in vast open savanna country.

We were allowed to feed the giraffes with straw. We were told that they had to get used to eating dried grass/hay because that is what they would get fed in the ships and their future homes. We stood on a high platform to feed the animals. The giraffe had a long thick tongue which came out and curled round the food before putting in into their mouth.

There had been talk in turning the Taton Island (Island of the Dead) in Tanga Harbour into a holding ground for the animals before being shipped overseas. As the story goes, there was not enough drinking water for the animals. So, in the end the animals were still shipped out via Voi, then Mombasa – Kenya.

*African Homes*

We had a chance to see how the Wa-Arusha lived among a tall banana grove in a round house with banana leaf doomed roof. While the Masai had long low homes made of wattle and mud and dung in open savanna country. With a few thorn trees.

Lovely for giraffes.

*Mount Meru*
A group of children had a chance to climb Mount Meru, I was not included. Shame!

*Pocket Money*
Every week we received one shilling (Sh) for pocket money. One week we could use it at the school tuckshop which was set up in one of the classrooms, or save it to use the next (2Sh) when we went to town to shop.

If we girls wanted to have a midnight feast, we would share our money to buy half a loaf of bread, quarter pound of butter, and jam. It was very important for us to slice the bread evenly with a pen knife, so that one day we could get married. Amazing how we did achieve it.

Sometimes I would buy a smoked kipper. Another time I bought from an African who was selling burnt things made from clay. I bought an ashtray with two birds, but this broke in the end, although I still have the little rabbit, which now has a broken leg.

One year the RSPCA came to the school and asked us children to join the organisation. We gave up our shilling, to be told we were now members of this body of people who help look after sick animals. Then we heard no more about the RSPCA, and we felt the teacher had helped us get rid of our money (No sweets that week).

Front school grounds. House in the background was on the other side of the river, and going to the river was the orchard and the lemon trees. Massowia and a cat.

## Polish Internees at Tengeru, near Arusha

As children in a boarding school one gets excited at any sort of entertainment by visiting people. One of my highlights was a group of Polish people who came to perform *Madam Butterfly*. There was singing in a language we did not understand, but that did not matter, for the one feature that has remained with me, were the beautiful costumes and the lightness of the fabric floating about in mingled colours of lilac, blue and more.

I must have been about 7/8 years old and one did not understand why these people were there. But years later on an island on Lake Kariba, Zimbabwe, a young Australian lady went rowing with one of my daughters, and she mentioned how she was in Arusha to learn more of her mother who had been in Tengeru. So we got speaking of my time at school, and I mentioned my memory of that delightful afternoon, sitting on the floor in the school dining room. She had spent six days in Arusha looking for information of those years her mother had been in Tengeru, but received nothing. I was happy to make her day, as she had something to go back home with of a little knowledge of her mother's time in Africa.

Now! Standing in a supermarket at Yiewsley, England, where I live, I asked a beautiful Somali lady if she was speaking Swahili from East Africa, and her reply was 'No', though I did pick up the odd Swahili word. I do not remember Swahili very well. Standing between us was a lovely elderly lady who informed us that she had been in Arusha as a refugee from Poland. Well! Massowia had to know more of their movement from Poland. I was invited to her home, where I learnt how the Russians came in the early hours and forced the family, who had military connections to leave their farms, to march off the east to become labourers in the 1920/30s. First working in forests, then always on the move, ending in Uzbekistan.

Then came the time in 1940/41 when the Poles were released by the Russians and were free, so the great hike making their way to Turkmenistan with the help of the Polish General Wladyslaw Andria, and with Sikorski/Maiski to make their way to the Caspian Sea, where some sailed from Krasnovodsk to Iran, or walked over the mountains from Ashgabat heading for Tehran, Persia. On arriving in Tehran, a lot of people were weak from starvation and illnesses. After a stay in Tehran for a while, transport of lorries which had been provided by Southern Rhodesia under the agreement of the Governors Conference of East Africa – Tanganyika, Uganda, Kenya, and Northern and Southern Rhodesia – they were transported to ships to be taken to Bombay (Mumbai), India, then by ships to Mombasa, Tanga, Dar-es-Salaam, Beira in Mozambique, Durban in South Africa. There were approximately 22,000 Poles for whom accommodation was required. Camps in Tanganyika were lfunda, Kidugala, Kigoma, Kondoa, Morogoro, and the largest settlement was Tengeru.

Lorries were the general form of transport for the refugees.

These camps were made up mainly with women and children and the men who were not fit enough to be enlisted into the British military forces of World War Two. The young women joined with the men into the forces. With all their moving about before coming to Africa a lot of the children were orphaned.

The Polish were given basic houses to live in. Kitchens were in other buildings or outside as well as the ablution blocks. The rest was left to them to become self supporting, like building churches, schools, and hospitals. Lots of gardens were made around the home too. Carpentry, mechanical working, farming. Fields for growing of crops and vegetables.

My delightful lady came with her sister and mother by ship to Dar es Salaam, and then by lorry to Njombe, then to Kidigala, lfunda. After a while they were moved to Tengeru in lorries, before going by Mombasa at the end of the war, then shipped to Southampton, England. A few Polish people went back to Poland, but the rest went to different parts of the world. The orphans went to New Zealand and Australia. My lady's husband had spent his time in India, before coming to England, where these two people met. Their homeland in East Poland had a new border and is now part of the Ukraine.

Living in London I had the chance to see *Madam Butterfly* performed at the Royal Albert Hall, London. It still holds a feeling of enjoyment and wonder.

In 1998 I had a privileged trip with a vet friend to go to Ashgabat, Turkmenistan to a Akhal-Teke horse conference. I had my own taxi and travelled about seeing an old town that had been destroyed many times over the centuries by earthquakes, whenever it was rebuilt. What an interesting time it was with its people and history.

## Kongwa

This amazing place called Kongwa. Home to the Wagogo people, who grew their millet, sorghum, maize, water melons, and other crops to feed the families and some to sell. Also herding of cattle. Millet is a grain of Africa, unlike maize which the Portuguese brought out of Mexico in the 1600s while sailing around the world. Millet grows well in a semi-arid environment. (It's an ideal food for the little black-masked love birds). Part of this central Tanganyika Territory (Tanzania) is a bleak dry area with lots of baobabs, thorny trees and scrub bush, which should have been left as it was.

The main town being Dodoma which the Germans wanted to make the capital. It now is the capital of Tanzania. Mpwapwa was the centre for the Church Missionary Society (CMS) from 1864 to

1874, also, the Dioceses for the Anglican Mission for East Africa. In the 1930s the government asked the Bishop at Mpwapwa to administer the running of the Arusha School for Europeans. Our great-grandfather Reverend Paul Ansorge in 1834/1854 who came from Silesia – Germany to Bengal – India, then Mauritius, was also a member of the CMS.

The Overseas Food Corporation (OFC) in 1946 started to build roads, a railway line from Msagali, going along the side of a range of hills to Kongwa, then on to Hogoro. This railway line only lasted from 1947 to 1952/3. I remember waking up in our cabin

when that train had stopped, it was still dark. We were told that an African had to walk in front of the train to check if the rail track had not been washed away by one of the dongas filling up with a flash of rain water. We were lucky, we could proceed to Kongwa. When, and if, the rains came these dongas could fill up quickly with water, otherwise they were dry river beds for most of the year.

A small airport was also built near the road leading from Kongwa to Hogoro.

Otherwise the main roads connecting Kongwa from Dar es Salaam, through Morogoro, Kilosa and onward through Kongwa to Buigri where there is a school for the blind, then onto Dodoma and beyond.

But what really happened due to the lack of food in Britain and Europe due to the end of the Second World War, was families were on rations. The British issued a mission to visit suitable sites to survey land for crop growing like sunflower and groundnuts in Africa. A certain gentleman by the name of Mr Frank Samual, head of the United African Company (UAC), part of the Unilever Company flew out to Tanganyika in the rainy season, and saw from the air, this vast country with the baobabs, and wondered why it had not been cultivated. People who were farming this difficult area were never consulted. So a team of people led by Mr John Wakefield from the Agricultural Department surveyed the place for three months and declared it suitable. Though I had heard the Germans wrote that area was not suitable for cultivation, due to lack of rain. The soil was clay and granite, which could turn into concrete, making it hard to reap crops like groundnuts. The best meteorological dates showed the region as a drought area in the country.

In 1946/1947, can you imagine the staff required for such an undertaking? The yer saw the arrival of tents used for housing and offices, while homes were being built for the 400 Europeans from around the world. I have not found out how the 5,500 labourers, mainly local people, were housed on the slopes of Kongwa Hill. Office foundations were built, but the walls were timber on the outside and hessian with cement and then white washed. Also workshops, club house built in the style of a Nissen building. Half way up was a high brick wall, the Nissen style corrugated iron roof. This was to become our dining room with the kitchen and storage rooms in the back, The boys had a converted office block as their dining area. A research station was also built. A hospital was built and equipped with the most modern equipment. Later this became the training centre for male nurses. Once we watched a play put on by the students and nursing staff. Full of fun and teasing, in Swahili and English. One joke I remember was: *Peleka Wagogo, Dodoma.* In Dodoma was the mental asylum.

A Junior School was built. Later, the buildings were used as a secondary school for Europeans after the collapse of the groundnut scheme in 1951. Before that Europeans were sent to Kenya for their secondary education. In fact the families now had a choice, either Kenya or Kongwa.

Equipment started to arrive for the clearing of the land. We were shown a film of Kongwa's beginning. Papers flying out of the tent office as a gust of wind blew through the tent. Well! We used to get the huge silent sand storms, with a "hooo" sounding noise as it approached going through all the buildings leaving sand on every thing.

Dar es Salaam Harbour at that time was not built for such volume of traffic of equipment, machinery, and heavy duty crawlers and tractors arriving from overseas, from such places like the Philippines, Canada, USA. It was expected that the main machinery was built in Leeds but could not be shipped out due to a fuel shortage. All one read about was a lot of delays, or railway lines washed away. But still they managed to get the equipment and other goods to arrive in Kongwa.

Though a lot of land had started with the cutting of the thorn trees, they still needed the crawlers to pull the very heavy ball and chain to help knock down the baobab trees. A few Africans were in the hollow of the trees: a sort of jail that the locals used. There were a lot of parakeets who loved to live in the hollow of these trees. Later this equipment and the ball and chain were sent to the Federation of Rhodesia and Nyasaland (now known as Zambia and Zimbabwe). I saw one of these chains marking a road to a house in Sengwa on a crocodile farm near Bumi Hills. This equipment was used to clear the land to build the Kariba dam.

Teachers' names -
1953 Coronation Book

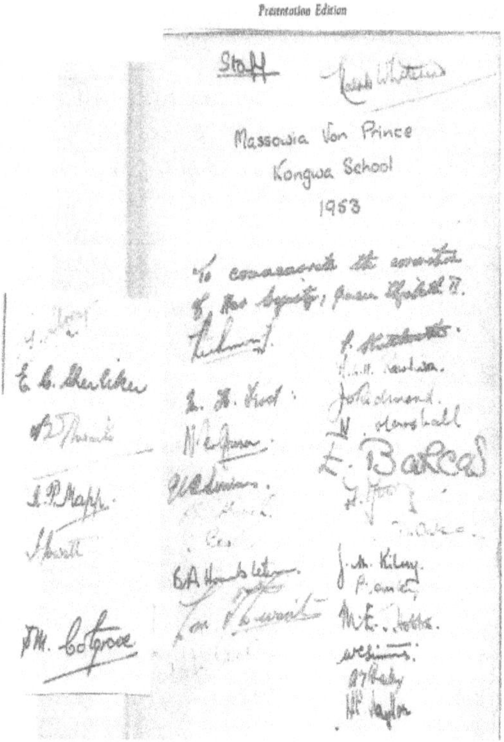

The Old OFC's office blocks.
Now classrooms. Massowia

Girls' house and kitchen
used by prefects. My flat
in 1957.

Original School building first used as dining room, gym, for school dances, etc

## KONGWA – TANGANYIKA - 1955

### Livingstone Girls

**Top Row:** Shiela MacDonald, Jacky Walker, Sandra Mansutti,
**Back Row:** Babel Grüniger, Massowia von Prince, Marie Eber, Mary Panayotakis, Ursala Grúniger, Hélenè Gregorious, Margarete Petifore,
**Middle Row:** Ann Vailey, Christa von Mutius, Edwina Milner, Eyvelen Wilson, Sílvia Middlem, Hanna Bayer, Nadia Aranky, Penny Collier, Linda Mitcheli-Hedges, Jean Ayton,
**Front Row:** Miss Rotcherson (Matron), Marilva ?, Daphine Kapprott, Miss Byless (House Mistress), Vicky Evdeman, Wilma Millner, Miss Bennington

The classroom buildings divided the residence. The bachelors used to live there. These homes became the boys' residence. The other side, where there was a tarred road and gravelly field, and rubber hedges were the married quarters. These became the girls' dormitory. There were four houses: Wilberforce, Nightingale, Currie and Livingstone. Livingstone was the name of my house. A long drop outside (toilet) and outer building which was once used as a kitchen.

Three of the kitchens were used as the sick bay, storage for our school trunks, and one used for prefects, housing two girls. It had a wash room. The fourth house was for the staff as their home.

The long drop toilet had other names: Thunderbox – here was a wooden platform with a hole, placed over the pit latrine. Swahili name *choo*. This was the one place after lights out in the main house, which had a light where we could go and study late into the night. The only flowers that seemed to grow on the outside were known as *choo* plants. Years later I was told they were periwinkles. A short woody plant – Madagascar Catharanthus rosen, with pink or white flowers. That it was a medicinal plant, using the bark of the roots for curing cancer. No wonder people did not understand *me* at first, as I only knew it as a *choo* flower.

The other exciting thing about this place was, that if you had to visit this building at night, there was often a chance you would meet up with a hyena, who happened to be visiting your garbage bin just outside the entrance door to the house. The only deference against these wild animals was to SCREAM. One night Evelyn Wilson met up with a cat, and she kindly sang to this pussy cat. 'If I knew you were coming, I would have baked a cake.'

There were many hyenas about, so the authorities set up round *bomas* made of cut scrub trees, and in the centre poisoned meat was placed. These animals were then used by the hospital for training students. Just to add, one year we even heard the roar of a lion.

We even collected chameleons as pets, mainly to bring into the dining room to eat the flies that used to fly in with us when we went for our lunch, or have them walk around the netting of our windows. These little creatures were often found in the manyara hedges. Oh! Yes. I must not forget the black faced parakeets that lived in the baobab trees.

The original building used as a general hall, dining and kitchen, before the closure of the groundnut scheme, was now used for the odd class project, like Shakespeare plays or geography classes. But! There was more to it. One of our teachers, when it was her weekend duty, her male friend would come from Dar es Salaam, to teach us square dancing while he played his fiddle and called out the various movements.

That was fun.

Nearby were the first classrooms built with verandas on either side of the glass classrooms. We did our secretary classes in Pitman's shorthand, typing and bookkeeping. For some reason this teacher did not like me, and we had a confrontation. I do not remember what it was, but she came to my desk and pulled out Black's Dictionary and wanted to hit my head with it. I jumped up and told the teacher to return the book to the draw. She was good at hitting me on the head. I won, but years later she got the better of me, on a math's subject I did not understand and she would not help me. I was sent outside, and a girl from another class started to talk to me. So I was brought in again, and still the lady refused to answer my question. She sent me to Mrs Gillam, Headmaster's wife, for my first ever six of the best. Mrs Gillam told me that the teacher was in the wrong, but I still had to have my canning. I was then a Prefect!!

While I was still in the B-stream we had domestic science, where we were taught to use electric and paraffin stoves. One thing I never managed was to make bread. Even when I was 50 years old and at a hotel school in Bournemouth. My tutor and another student made sure I would make good bread rolls. They made lovely round rolls, But, when they demonstrated to me, their rolls were a flop. I was jinxed.

Dining room or mess: the boys had one of the long office blocks, while we girls had the old club house in the form of a Nissan hut (a prefabricated steel and corrugated structure also using bricks). The tennis courts were near the club house, and it was where we had our end of the year dance night, or during the day you could play tennis. Something I could never learn to play well. Squash was more my scene.

We had assembly outside one of the blocks of classes. This is where we had out-of-door cinema or film shows when people came to talk to us about how the Bible was made up of different collections of texts. Or, another time a man came and showed slides on the Kondoa lrangi Rock Paintings near the Great North Road between Dodoma and Arusha. It was pointed out that these paintings can be found from the Sahara to South Africa.

The swimming pool was by the new Club House. Usually it was a long run from the classrooms for our swimming lessons. There various activities relating to swimming, such as the usual swimming competition. Water polo, I enjoyed that. Then Miss Frost taught us lifesaving and first aid. I could not go beyond the bronze medal, as I found it hard to dive from the 10 foot board. No problem to dive from stacked-up chairs, but 10 foot, that was another story. The first aid I enjoyed as I found I could use the knowledge when I married and moved to Southern Rhodesia on a farm, and could help the workers and their families.

Miss Taylor, our music teacher, was really good. In classes she introduced us to classic music and understanding of the great musicians, also explaining the various instruments used in an orchestra. But best of all, was learning the songs from Gilbert and Sullivan, such as *Pirates of Penzance*, *Mikado*, and *Trial by Jury*, this we performed on the stage of the Dodoma cinema house.

The whole school took part. Boys in carpentry classes built the stage, while the girls sewed costumes. We made paper flowers. But the teachers were a great help, making wigs and props. It was a busy time. This happened in our first term of the year, and the second was singing carols at the Dodoma Cathedral.

Our transport was sitting on dining benches in open lorries. And there was I with my long hair rolled in bandages to create ringlets, which at the end of the day was not that good, for the *Trial by Jury*. We had a meal in the hotel, but the second term was to private peoples' homes. When we got back to school, about one o'clock in the morning, we had a warm drink before making our way in the dark to our houses.

The singing of some of the boys and girls was really good. I remember Nana Rigas had an especially strong voice and could reach the high notes.

Judges' Court

The props were made by the boys in their carpentry class with a Catholic Father who gave the lessons.

The Bride and Bride's Maids' clothes and flowers were made in domestic class.

Teachers helped make other items such as wigs.

Bride in Court - Rodger, Walter, Bride Jackie Walker, Etuis, Jackie W, Ron, Augisa

Bride's Maids - Coring, Susie, Franka, Rosaria, Jackie W, Dawn, Sheila, Massowia, Yola

The Jury including Mr Whitehead sitting in the back

The public, sorry no names, but must mention that the short girl standing behind the Clerk is Nina Rigas. She had the most amazing voice and could hit the high notes.

I can still remember we had some Seychelles girls with their dark glossy hair playing the piano. Any new pop song that came on the radio, they could play, and we would have a sing song around the piano. Miss Taylor mentioned to me that she had to spend the extra time teaching them as it was going to be their profession.

Sport! Well, what can I say? We girls learned lacrosse. This we had for one term, as Kongwa was too hot for such an energy game. Too much running around. Then, the normal games like hockey – I usually played both wings. Netball and rounders. Tennis – I was never good, but, better with squash. The walls of an old building were used with the roof removed. Athletics, we would compete between the houses. I enjoyed the javelin or long distance running. Swimming was another competitive sport. All I remember were the boys playing rugby and at times another school would come to compete. I am not sure what other sport the boys played. One thing, Kongwa was so dry, there was no grass, only just a little around the school buildings as grass oblong beds surrounded by stone, always green. The playing fields were just gravel.

Athletic team

Massowia throwing the javlin

Miss Frost watching with us a visiting team

Girls at the swimming club.

Do you know who is swimming?

Road sign outside the Units. With Massowia, Helga and Hanna.

## Units

Another trip was out to the Units (as the groundnut fields were called) to the Research Station. To see how the weather is measured with the various weather equipment. Also, to see the various grasses grown to see what would be best for cattle ranching, which used the cleared groundnut fields for grazing. I remember them mentioning the best grass came from Southern Rhodesia. It was known that the best beef came from Kongwa.

We seemed to really have a wild time in this bush school. I loved it, though there were days which were otherwise, because the school was so spread out. I wandered to the Mission Hospital at the foot hills of the mountains, and here I saw newly born babies. Once you reached your last year of school, you could go out of the school grounds for picnics at the half term. We were able to borrow bikes from the boys, and off to the Units we went for our picnics. I used to carry the water bottles in a *kikapu* (woven basket tied to the bike handle). We would rest by the shade of the manyara (rubber) hedge, climb the thorny trees growing in sandy river beds. Hanna lent me her bike and that was when I learnt to ride. One day I got into trouble with the matron, as I practised during our rest period after lunch.

In my last year I was a prefect for a second year and I had the privilege of having the kitchen as my accommodation with another girl. We had our own wash room, but still had to go to the main house for a bath. We decorated the room with paintings from songs like 'Red Sails in the Sunset'. We had a walk-in cupboard. Father made me a little stove from a round tin, using cotton wool and spirit. I had a small pot. Wednesday was butcher's day at the village, where fresh meat could be bought. If there were no babies, matron would bring back brain for me to cook on my small cooker. I have always loved the taste of brain.

When I first came to Kongwa, Bridget (Biddy or Chip) Goodrich was there. I have known the family from Tanga, She is two years my senior. Something I never knew, but she pointed out to her friends I had a patch of white hair.

Hanna and Marjolein cooking toffee by the 45 gallon drum which boiled our bath.

Sandra

Hanna and Marjolein near the tennis courts, coming from the girls' dining mess.

Livingstone Girls with Penny Collier having fun.

Helene and Hanna

Massowia outside her flat. We were allowed to make our own gardens

Edwina at the cross roads on the way either to the classrooms or girls' houses.

Above: Hanna, Anita, Reinhold, Helga
Left: Hanna, Anita, Reinhold, Helga
Below right: Hanna, Reinhold, Massowia with water bottle basket
Below left: With the cattle out in the Units with Reinhold, Anita, Helga, Hanna

Reinhold Waltenberg - Head Girl

Hanna Bayer

Anita Hall

**Pen Friend**

Johnny phoned me in the 1970s. She was then married to a Mr Smith who was working with the Post Office, asking how we were, but was not allowed to give me her address.

My pen friend Johnny Kay with her brother. We kept in touch until 1969.

*Buigiri blind school*

Trips away from the school included one to Buigiri, where there was a school for the blind on the road to Dodoma which opened in 1950. We watched them make baskets and other things from the striped baobab bark. At that time the Government Optician travelled around Tanganyika. When I met this man in Tanga for an eye test, I mentioned this school. He explained the hard time he had teaching the people to grow more yellow foods for the families to stop the development of blindness.

Painting of Massowia by Ernst von Glasow, a cousin

# German Trip to Meet the Family ~ 1955

For me, my trip started with having my passport photo taken at Kongwa School in my school uniform, with a green blanket as the background. As things are when in boarding school the parents had to ask the school to attend to various requests on their behalf. I was fifteen and a half years old. My sister was seven years.

After our musical performance of *Trial By Jury* by Gilbert and Sullivan at the Dodoma Cinema, I was taken to the Railway Station for my trip back to Tanga, where I was met by my mother and sister, Frederica. What amazes me today was how we youngsters could travel on our own in complete safety all those years ago. This trip was the train to Morogoro, railway bus to Korogwe, then train to Tanga, There would always be a conductor to keep an eye on you to make sure you were on the correct route to your destination.

Once home, I was surprised to see Father in bed with his hand bandage up. Father had found another type of extremely hard wood. He was planning this piece of wood on the electric planner when the wood slipped out and smashed his two little fingers. We were lucky that Dad had his assistant, Danny Nortjie, working for us and he was left to look after Father. Danny was a real happy chappie.

We got ready for this trip to Germany. Mother had not seen her mother Marianne Siems nee Claus since 1937 when Mum left for Tanga/Korogwe, Tanganyika to marry Dad, Massow von Prince on 5 June 1937 in Korogwe.

Well, we then flew out of Tanga on a Dakota plane to Nairobi, Kenya, where we connected to our flight for Frankfort, Germany with the SAS (Scandinavian Airline Services). Our first stop out of Nairobi was Khartoum – Sudan. Here we spent a very hot night at the airport. Then next day we hopped to Rome – Italy, then to Zurich – Switzerland and met up with Mother's uncle, Herbert Esche. (He gave mother as a wedding a present a beautiful two twisted gold chain which I still enjoy wearing.)

On our arrival in Frankfort-am-Maine, Father's first born, my half-brother Hanson was with his divorced wife Anne (lovely lady), and Mother's childhood friend from the time they were four years old, *Tante* Dollie Gaitch.

Anne wanted to get to know mother, as Hanson had custody of Tom and Uta. (Poor small children, both under four years). These two children would be coming out to Africa to live with us. We then spent some time in the park with the family.

Our hotel was near the railway station. One could still see the effect of the Second World War. It was bewildering for me lacking knowledge of the German language. We could not drink the water, unless you drank soda water (which I could not as it gave me a headache straight away).

There was still a problem with the infrastructure due to the bombing, as a lot of damage was done. We could only get boiled water to drink from the railway station, and had to wait until after ten o'clock in the morning.

Across from the hotel was a restaurant where we had our evening meal. By then we were alone with *Tante* Dolle. This evening was so amusing, seeing those two ladies behaving like children, catching up on their eighteen years of not seeing each other. In the end the Restaurant Manager asked them to behave and keep their voices down, as they were also laughing a lot and really enjoying themselves. I was surprised to see Mother in this childish state with her friend and it was lovely. In the end we were asked to leave in disgrace.

A day later we made our way by train to Ebnath. The nearest rail station to Ebnath seems to be Neusorg. I really do not know. We were met by Uncle Ivan von Peterffy. The family were living in the Forsthaus. The others being Erica, mother's sister and her daughter Ester. Uncle Oktav von Peterffy, brother of Uncle Ivan. Agnes, granny's maid. Downstairs were the Simons. Their son Wolfgang was later to marry Ester. Upstairs in Granny's room we met this elderly lady. I was shocked to see my mother meeting up with her mother. Mother got on the floor and with her head on her mother's lap she was crying while Frederica and I were looking on, at this very emotional scene. Our rooms were on the third floor. At one time Mother and Frederica felt the cold and slept under feather duvets. I found it hot. We stayed awhile. I remember Uncle Ivan took us to see a doctor to remove my in-growing warts which I picked up at school. Well the first doctor I saw said to me as I came from Africa I would not feel any pain. I had to sit on a wired padded type of cushion and he proceeded to cut deeply into this offending wart. I kept quiet. Well the second time I went to him Uncle came and told the doctor off and this time he numbed the area. Uncle threatened him that he would take Granny's business away. Granny had damaged her knees while she was in a Russian camp. The prisoners had to collect wood for the fire from the forests. If they did not have enough wood they would not be fed. Uncle Oktav who had once been a Minister in the Hungarian parliament managed to find Granny and he told the authorities he had been looking for his wife, and so saved Granny.

Our trips around the three western zones, we ended up coming back to Ebnath. So back on the train to Hamburg, this time to Father's second child, Uta Topp our half-sister. From the train we saw people working in the fields and harvesting wheat and other crops. And always people waving. At some of the stations people would sell Frankfurters on a plate with a big dollop of mustard. Money was tight and I could see it on Mother's face when we begged for more, but still she relented. Dear Mother.

## Hamburg

Our long train trip from Ebnath found us with my half-sister Uta Topp and her family living at Faberstasse, Hamburg 19. It was good to see Uta again. The last time was when she was a single lady and came to Tanga to visit her father.

One of the first things we did was to visit a doctor to operate on my foot to remove the in-growing wart, which had grown for the third time. It was very painful to walk.

A trip to the *Tierpark*, Hagenbeck (Zoo). The Hagenbeck family started collecting animals from around the world in the 1800s, which Carl Hagenbeck Jr started as a Zoo which in 1907 opened with moats being built so the animals could be taken out of cages and could then roam freely in the park. I was fascinated with this history, as it was the first of its kind in the world.

Sightseeing around the harbour, you will see the three of us by the pole on the boat. I saw a large sailing ship. These sailing ships are used for training sailors. Amazing how busy and big the harbour was compared to our little harbour in Tanga, All those railway lines and waterways for trains and ocean-going ships.

We went to the shopping centre (Alstorokaden) and the Rathaus, which brought happy memories for my darling Mother and her young days before the Second World War.

There was a lot to see. Poor Frederica, one day she was so tired that she just sat in the middle of the road and stopped the traffic. Also one time on the train heading for Ebnath, Frederica was not well and sitting on Mum's lap, when a German woman told Mother off for having her daughter on her lap and Mother begging to be allowed to look after her child, and being told that the child had to stand, even if she was that ill and could not stand.

After Hamburg we continued our trip. This time with Hanson.

## Rhine and Lauterecken

Now, our continued travels after leaving Hamburg with a car is a little of a mix as I do not remember how we were with Hanson again, where we stayed the nights and with whom. We went to many interesting places, starting in Cologne (Koln), and we visited that fantastic Roman Catholic Cathedral. Construction started from 1248. I cannot help mentioning 4711 Eau de Cologne. Beautiful present to give, especially people in hospitals.

Then, we were in Berg Eltz by the Mosel River. We did not stop long there before heading for Coblenz (Koblenz), on the cross roads of the Mosel and Rhine Rivers. We went up to the Fort; from there one could see for miles, also watch the trading and tourist ships moving along these huge rivers. Here Hanson explained all the films made were stored in the hill, as the air was dry. He explained damp air would damage the films. From the top we looked across to the area where the Mosel meets the Rhine and there was an empty stand where once stood the monument of Emperor William I on his horse. The statue disappeared one night, and was never found.

Travelling down the Rhine, the day was beautiful and the scenery with so many historical sights, like an Island in the old times, traders had to pay toll fees to enable them to proceed up or down the river. We saw musical and dancing festivals in some of the towns we passed. But what I remembered most was eating cherries. There again poor Mother, we begged her for more. By the look on her face I could see they were expensive, but we youngsters did not seem to care.

In between us meandering our way to Hanson's place, we stopped by visiting family. There was cousin Frederica von Glassow (Frederica kept her maiden name). We met her son Michael, also *Tante* Lotte came. But the first time we saw Charlotte von Glassow, she was working for a lady younger than herself. It shocked me to realise that she had lost her home in East Germany where she lived in huge manor homes with servants. All she had was a bedroom in this lady's home. With this knowledge it has been a lesson to me, that if you lose everything you can still make a life for yourself. Then there was *Tante* Ang (Angelka) von Lobbecke with her daughter (cousin) Putty (Margarete). Dear old *Tante* Ang loved to smoke and she took me to a corner of the room to show me how she lit her cigarette by splicing the end before lighting it so it could catch the flame quicker. Mother and daughter shared the room. Both these *Tantes* were sisters of our grandmother Magdalene von Prince nee von Massow.

We spent a week or so with Hanson and Thomas, at his home in Lauterecken.

Hanson had to go back to work. He worked for the American Army at the time. It was here that I met Else his second wife to be.

From there we went to Munich to Mother's sister Irene Szalla.

## Daren /Vechta – British Zone

Parting company with Mother in Nuremberg, I was heading north to the Artist Ernest von Glasow, as he was commissioned by Margarete (Putty) von Lobbecke to paint my portrait. I was with him and his family for a few days. As most of my time was spent sitting, I did not get to know the others very well.

A man on the train told me I would get to Vechta quicker if we changed trains. I was informed that he had been a prisoner of war in England, and as he spoke good English, he was given the job as interpreter. I followed his guidance, so I do not remember which station we got off at, to wait for the next train. When our train arrived it did not stop at the station itself, but a little to the side. When we got on the train there was no seating available, on account of it was full of orphaned children from East Germany, and we had Russian soldiers guarding the train. For me it was a sad sight to see these young people with a brown card with their name and other details on hanging around their necks, and carrying a small brown case. When I think of it, I can see clearly the dead pan look in those children's eyes.

As you can imagine I was late when I arrived at Vechta. The family had been and gone, so the Station Master told me where I could bed down for the night. The woman at this hostile asked for my passport and went on questioning me about it. I told her I did not know what she was saying as I spoke no German. By now in Germany I had learnt to understand some German, and realized she was saying that my Visa had expired. So I took my pass and paid her, then went to a dark room as directed and slept in a filthy bed.

Back at the station next morning, I got onto a local wooden body carriage, and we set off, going 'Ping-a-ling Ping-a-ling' along the rail. We stopped outside a house and I was told to jump down as that was the stop and the conductor pointed out where I was to go. Lucky for me I came across Michael – Frederica von Glasow's son, with other boys. So I was taken to Uncle Ernest, who was busy with his onions. He grew them to earn more money.

So my days were spent sitting for the painting. But one day the youngsters took me to the fair. I remembered just really enjoy it, especially the little cars. I had now lost control and spent my time laughing. To get to Vechta we went by bike, and it took a little while to get used to peddling backwards, as that was the break system. We hid the bikes in a field and in the hay stacks. On our way back we were stopped by the Police and I was told to stay in the back and not say a word. It was dark and only one bike had a light.

Then I was back on the train to Ebnath. No mishap this time.

## Ebnath – USA zone

Making my way back to Ebnath, after spending time traveling about from Hamburg to the Mosel/Rhine, Koblenz (Coblenz) traveling down the Rhine before crossing over to Lauterecken with Hanson to his home, it is here that I met Elsa, Hanson's future wife.

Somehow I find myself in Bavaria again at such places as Berchtesgaden and Munich with family for about three weeks. At the end of my stay with Aunt Irene, Hanson's mother, I was again on the train heading for East Germany and the border post of West and East Germany in 1955 – Hof. When I arrived at the station, looking through the window of the train, I saw the worried face of my Mother and Uncle Ivan. It was to do in case I did not wake up and found myself in East Germany. They would have had a hard time getting me back. (Shame!) Lucky I was not asleep, it was a long journey.

First day back with Granny and at the meal table, I was told not to speak with an American accent, as she would not have that language spoken in her home, so I kept my mouth shut. Until one day Granny was reading to me in German. A book on how young ladies had to know how to behave in society. Then Granny asked why I was not talking to her, my reply was I was forbidden to speak with an American accent, which I did not know I had picked up.

The home was known as the Forsthaus by the river Fichtelnaab. I went swimming with Fidi. It was here that we often spoke with each other in Swahili so others could not know what was said. Surrounding the town were farm lands and forest. The forest was managed by the family and another family working with Uncle Ivan.

The village life was interesting with the sound of church bells and bird song. Or going very early to the baker to buy freshly baked rolls for breakfast. Seeing homes with cattle stalls on the ground floor while upstairs the family lived. I was told it was one way to keep the home warm for winter.

The one thing that really upset me was to see the Euroasian

Uhu (Eagle Owl) bubo bubo kept caged in an open cave-like home, to be fed by the wild cats that were shot. It was explained that they had workers going about the forest to shoot the wild cats that were devastating the bird population. The Uhu being the largest owl in the world is a most proud looking bird. But the eyes looked sad.

It was also the time that Aunt Erica and Ester were busy harvesting their vegetable crops for canning/bottling for storage for the winter. These they had grown in their side garden, some under glass. There was this big cellar below ground where food was stored like potatoes, apples, or whatever.

Men had been hunting for deer which was hung in a shed for a week before it was prepared, also for winter food.

Uncle Octav, Uncle Ivan's brother who was retired often took me for walks in the forests looking for mushrooms and pointing out areas of open ground. Sometimes we would see a deer in these openings. This is where my interest of mushrooms was born. I learnt so much from this lovely gently Old Man (as I would call him). He also interested me in stamp collecting.

There was a boy who was visiting his family whose uncle was working with Uncle Ivan with forest business. Years later his cousin, who married my cousin Ester, reminded me of showing his cousin a knife game which we used to play in Kongwa School.

So after a good rest Mother and I were on the road again. This time Fidi stayed with the family. Mother went to the other family and also to the Bodensee (Lake Constance). We travelled to Nuremberg by train and we split company and I went north.

## Munich

During our time in Munich with Mother and her third sister, Irene Szalla, Frederica and I were shown lots of interesting places. I did not know what these ladies were protecting us from. One museum was full of naked statues from Greek and Roman times. Not a sight for young ladies. I was fifteen years old and my sister was seven years. They should have seen how the Maasi and Warusha dressed with just a cloth tied across their one shoulder and with the movement of their walk and winds flapping their cloth open. Okay they did wear a leather belt with leather holder attached to the belt which held their panga, but still?

As *Tante* Irene was working, Fidi and I went with Mother to see the Nymphenburg Palace to see the hand manufacturing of the Nymphenburg Porcelain which was started sometime in the 1750s using an old recipe made from raw materials of kaolin, feldspar and quartz, taking two days to mix to the right consistency. The mixture was worked into blocks which were stored in very cool cells, and kept moist so the clay would not dry out. I remember them mentioning the longer the clay was stored to mature the finer porcelain one would have.

Then we were taken to see the porcelain turned into objects. Then the kiln firing. What really fascinated me was seeing the lady adding a little white rubber into the clay to hold it together to turn into fine petals for flowers such as roses and other very fine objects, then added to whatever object to complete the subject. But the dainty roses have always remained with me and the fine net dipped into porcelain sludge for dressing on the figurines models. The dainty painting showing how realistic it all looked.

When decorating a birthday cake for my daughter Anita years later, I dipped a net into royal icing to create a long lacy skirt for the marzipan bride doll.

I then spent about two weeks alone with *Tante* Irene, who went during the day to work for her Macaroni Man. Most of the time I was left to my own devices. One weekend *Tante* Irene had time off and we went together to the Chiemsee Lake, south-east of Munich to see the Herrenchiemsee Palace on the Herreninsel (Island). Another Palace of King Ludwig II. The park with forests on either side of the designed garden with a water way up the middle with many fountains leading up to the Palace. But the largest of the fountains was a big round tiered fountain with many frogs spouting water. All too beautiful.

This time I went on my own by coach to the village of Hohenswangau at the foot of the castle to see the all gleaming white Neushwanstein Castle on top of a steep hill. (You could translate the name as New Swan Stone). It was a long walk up to this fairytale castle. It was mind boggling for me coming from Africa and bush mud huts with thatched roofs, and anything as new to buildings of our churches in Africa with their artistic designs. But NO where at all near in beauty to these palaces and churches in Europe.

I bought a book for Father about King Ludwig II, but he was not impressed. Oh well. Also bought lunch, the result was I did not have enough change for my return tram trip to my Aunt's home at Winthirststrasse. As I did not have her telephone number and lucky it was a hot sunny July day, I followed the tram line to Rotkranzplatz (Red Cross Square) on the cross roads of Leonrodstrasse and Nymphenburg Road. Having arrived at the coach station at about 18.00 hours, it took me nearly four hours to get home. All I remembered was that the tram had many bends for me to follow. It taught me to pay attention to foreign money after that.

Coming from Africa I was amazed to hear how people were dying from the very hot July weather, especially the elderly. Some of the young people lying sunbathing also died.

Another place I went with Mother was the English Gardens. A beautiful park with trees and lakes near the centre of the city. Mother mentioned that when Father was working in Munich and did not have money he would sleep on the benches and feed himself with a tablespoon of cod liver oil. It was a good place to go again when I was on my own.

Aunt Irene also rented out a room to a Yugoslavian lady who was making plans to marry a man from Argentina, as she said it was her chance to get out of Europe. She was a beautiful dark haired girl.

Did not get much chance to learn German as all the people wanted to learn English, especially the girls in the shops as they were hoping for a date with the American soldiers. We young people with starry eyes.

## Berchtesgaden

A visit to Berchtesgaden to meet Hanson and Uta's mother, Irene. My father's first wife living with old friends of my father. (I seem to remember the name von Schorn, but then 1955?) I remember the home was on a sloop of a hill with lots of open ground. From here the view was wonderful as you could see the Watzman Mountain. Father walked it in one day. To prove to his friends, he went up again in one day.

Irene treated me to three trips all lovely and interesting. The Kongesee, a crystal clear lake nestling between very high and steep cliffs. The only way to get to the famous St Bartholomew, the Apostle patron to the Alpine farmers and dairymen. The red onion domes atop its ancient pilgrimage church on the peninsular. The east side of the lake you can see the east face of the Watzman Mountain. One can reach this church also by going over the mountain, but no cars are allowed.

A day coach trip to Salzburg, Austria. We nearly did not go through the border as I did not have a visa on my British Passport. What Irene made of it, but we were allowed through. We walked up to the Prince-Archbishops castle. Before going back to Germany we had a lovely, sunny, walk along the river.

But, best and interesting was the Salt Mine, SalzZeitReisen. We all had to wear protective clothing and were given leather aprons to wear to protect our backside, for when we had to slide the wood shoots. We started our trip sitting astride a bench like train to go into the mine, then, we went sliding down the wooden shoots to the salt lake with is crystal clear water. Then we got onto a raft to move to the other side. And somehow we ended up at the gift shop, where I bought a box of mixed coloured salts as a gift for Father. The tour was conducted in German so I did not understand what was said. What was a little sad for me, was, Irene would not allow the young men to talk to me. They were cheerful, full of fun, and good looking. Irene sat behind me.

## Towards the end of my trip

Some time while at Ebnath, Mother took us to the St Emmeram Palace of the noble family Thurn und Taxis in the area of Regensburg. The art work in the chapel was fantastic. It was here mother mentioned that the family gave their name to the Taxi hiring companies.

After my last week in Ebnath, I made the train trip on my own to Frankfort-am-Maine, where Hanson met me and took me to the airport for my return trip to Africa. On arriving in Nairobi, Kenya Airport, my case went missing. I was bringing family silver in the case and hand case wrapped in my clothes. I then saw the brown case in a dark corner in the customs room. I had declared the silver and mentioned it was a gift from my grand-mother and I did not know the value as I would not be rude enough to ask such a question from an elderly lady, as she knew I was coming to Africa. In the meantime the small coach that was to take us to the Norfolk Hotel was getting impatient, where I stayed the night.

I asked the reception at the Norfolk Hotel to wake me up so that I would be awake for my transport to take me to the airport for my final fight to Tanga, where my father met me. The Hotel reception never woke me, and when I came down the stairs there was my driver waiting for me.

Having a few days at home and getting my school things packed, Father took me by car to Kongwa via Morogoro, Kilosa, then school. Miss Frost was a good friend to me from Arusha and Kongwa schools. Miss Frost made one visit us in Tanga. It was here that Dad stayed with her for a day or two before going back to Tanga.

I left school with long hair and returned with a short haircut, which was cut for me when we arrived in Frankfort.

Arrival in Frankfurt

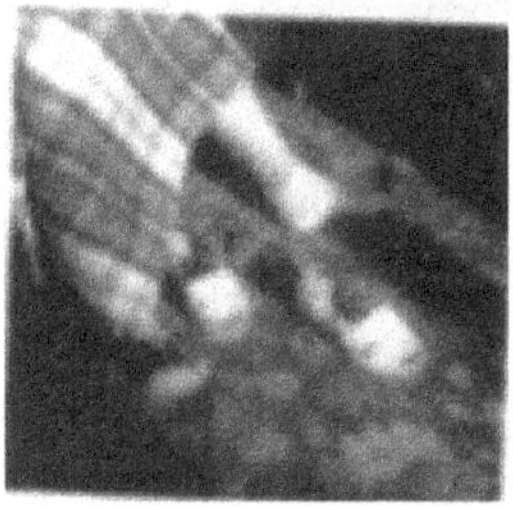

Above: Grounded
Left: Harbour trip
Bottom left: *Tierpark*, Hagenbeck
Below: Alstorokaden shopping centre

Top left: Frederica with her mother Charlotte von Glassow
Top right: Frederica, Massowia, Margarete, Frederica jr, Tom, Hanson - at Frederica's house
Various family members
Left and below: Ebnath - Forstaus
Frederica with buck

Entrance to Koln Cathedral
Rhine River with Castles

Left and below: The Mosel and Rhine at Coblenz. Emperor monument of Emperor Wilhelm 1 and Fort, Berg Eltz

Berchtesgaden
SalzZeitReisen - Massowia is fourth from the front and behind Irene von Prince

The end of the trip

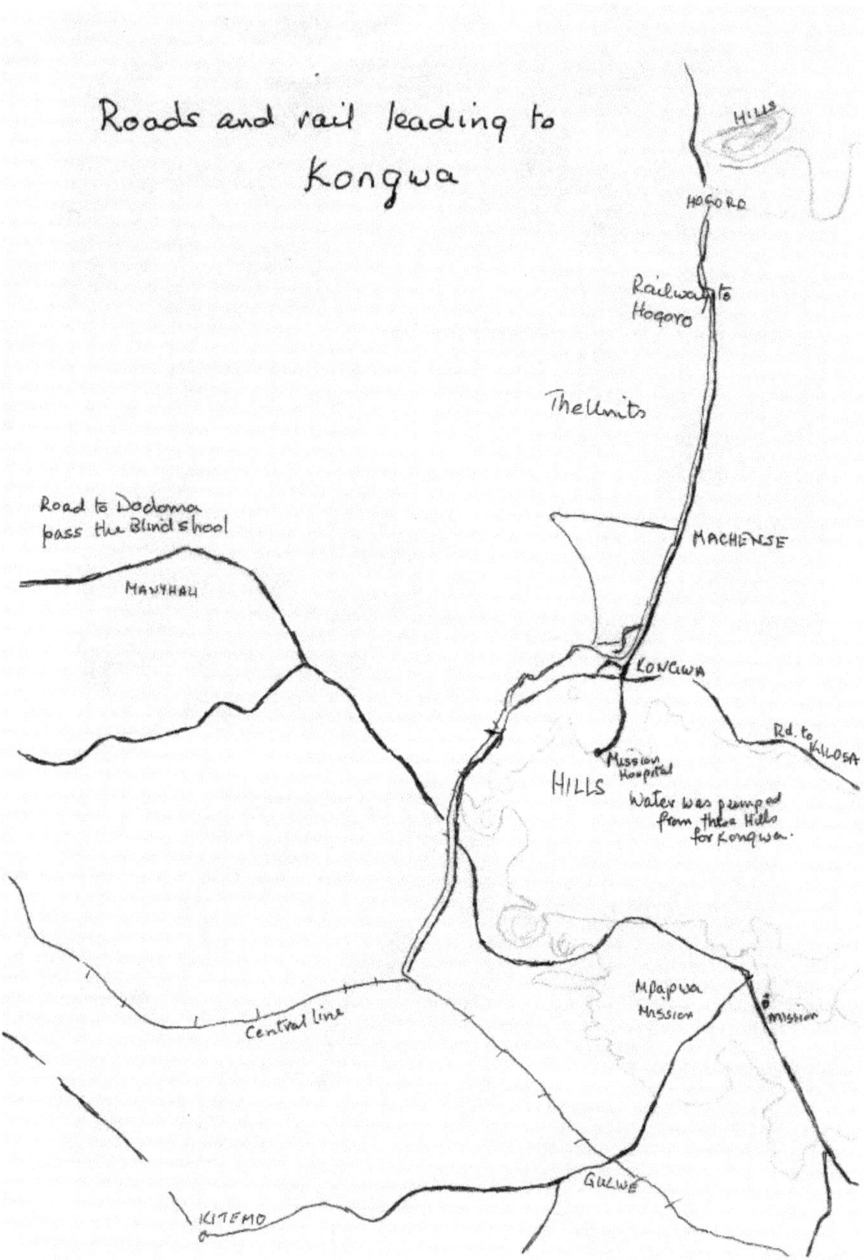
Roads and rail leading to Kongwa
HILLS
HOGORO
Railway to Hogoro
TheUnits
Road to Dodoma pass the Blind shool
MACHENSE
MANYHALI
KONGWA
Rd. to KILOSA
Mission Hospital
HILLS
Water was pumped from these Hills for Kongwa.
Mpapwa Mission
MISSION
Central Line
GULWE
KITEMO

# Trains

## Gari La Moshi – (Smoking Vehicle!)

My school day's transport from home to Lushoto was by car. But going to Arushas and Kongwe, it was TRAINS, RAILWAY BUSES or lorries. Distances were great. We would find ourselves sleeping on bunks in the trains, also having our meals in the train. Except on our return road trip from Morogoro., when we arrived back in Korogwe and were taken to the hotel for a meal, there to greet us was a row of chairs with men sitting with the baggy khaki shorts and legs apart for all to see what they possessed as we filled past. (No underpants.)

Once the train did not go to Kongwa, we then went on to Dodoma, it was lorries to Kongwa School. The reason was that after the train would branch off on our way to Kongwa, a man had to walk in front of the train after heavy rains (average 20 inches of rain) as the *korongos* (gullies) could fill with water and wash the railway bridge away.

Seeing these hug Garrett Engines pulling all the carriages along the savannah or bush land and crossing rivers, as we stuck our heads out of the windows we would get a blast of sooty smoke, if the wind was at the right angle to blow the smoke along the carriages. But seeing the train travelling along on the rails, it reminded us of a large black millipede (Diplopodo) (Swahili – *jongoo*). Between Moshi and Arusha one looked towards snow topped Mount Kilimanjaro, on the plain we would often see Thomson's Gazelles.

Zanzibar had its first tram line about 1881. But seeing old photographs there were tram lines in Tanga and Dar es Salaam. In 1891 the Germans started to build their first railway line from Tanga to Moshi and completed it in September 1911, known as the Usambara Railway. It was a time that Greeks were employed as overseers/foremen (Swahili – *msimamizi*) in the building of the rail line. There were branches which led from the main line. Also there were points made for future lines to be built to other destinations.

Tanga to Muheza, a town you took by road up the Eastern Usambara to Amani. But the next station at Tengeni was a steam train known as Sigi-Bahn working on a pulley system to the Research Station in Amani, where there was a big Water Wheel generating power for pulling the train up the mountain. Father (Massow) took me there and explained how the system worked. One could still see the water wheel and buildings. Massow pointed out the wild red bananas which produced seeds, and mentioned that they only grew in two places, here in the Eastern Usambaras and on Mount Elgen in Kenya/Uganda. I saw coffee trees that had gone wild and were as tall as forest trees. Also Father pointed out the very tall camphor trees. This timber used for making boxes and furniture. It could be sawn very thinly to make cigar boxes. The camphor smell kept the insects away.

At the Murasi Junction it was planned to join the Usambara Line to the Central line from Dar es Salaam to Kigoma via Ujiji at Ruvu. (The railway line was later built in 1977).

So we go on to Korogwe, a meeting place of two rivers – Pagani and the Lwengara Valley and river that divided the East and West Usambara Mountains. Not only the rivers met here but the Handeni/Morogoro road. This town was in a very swampy area with lots of mosquitoes. I noticed a lot of people had Elephantiasis (Lymphatic filariasis). Their legs were very swollen.

Traveling onwards to Mombo. Here is a road leading you to the top of the Usambaras, passing Soni, Soni Falls and Hotel, then onto Lushoto Town, once known as Wilhelmstal in German times. There were many interesting places, like the World View and on a clear day one could see Mount Kilimanjaro. Due to the sawmills in the forests of that area, a cable way was installed to move timber to the railway line at Mkumbara Station. It was known as the Seilbahn from Adolf Bleichert & Co. in 1910. In the 1950s it was still working when I was there with the family. The Lutheran Mission centre at Moi, the White Fathers and their mission at Sakarani, where Tom and Magdalene von Prince had their coffee estate before World War One.

There were the Lushoto and St Michael's School, also Mission Schools for the locals.

So back to Mombo to join the train heading to Moshi, but before we reach Moshi, at Kahe Junction was the plan to join the railway to Voi on the Uganda Railway in Kenya. This railway line connected the towns of Mombasa, Nairobi, and onwards to Uganda.

Moshi was an important town with its coffee plantations on and around Mount Kilimanjaro. I was once told there were about 25 different type of bananas. The road and rail system going between Moshi and Arusha joined to the Great North Road. Then via Moshi to Voi in Kenya and then to Tanga. The Arusha railway line connection was put on hold due to the start of World War One, but after the war the building of the rail line commenced and was completed in 1930.

This railway line was useful for transporting live wild animals to the zoos, which took the animals via Voi, then onto Mombasa and shipped out world wide.

The other train one travelled on was once known as the *Mittlland Bahn* (German for Central line). This railway followed the old Arab trade caravan route from Lake Tanganyika to the coast at Bagamoyo and Dar es Salaam. The Germans started laying the railway line from Dar es Salaam, which happened to be the shipping harbour as well as the capital, to Lake Tanganyika in 1904, which was completed in February 1914.

Like the Usambabra Railway, there were other junctions, like the planned route from Ruvu to Murasi. (This line was built in 1977). At Morogoro the road from Korgowe/Handeni joined with the main rail line and roads to Kilosa, Mpapwa, Dodoma, and beyond.

All I can say is that during the rainy season this road with its deep red muddy soil, one had to be careful not to get stuck in the mud. Once we had to get out of the Railway Bus to push the bus out. Often one could see a lorry on its side, or car truly stuck in the mud.

There at Kilosa Junction was a line to Kitadu. Then back to the main line going to the next junction at Msagali, took the railway to Hororo in 1948. This had been in connection with the groundnut scheme in Kongwa and the Units. Part of the line was closed in 1951, then 1954 to Kongwa.

When reaching Dodoma, this was the junction connection with the Great North Road from Rhodesia to Kenya. This town the Germans had hoped to make the capital. From here we went on to Tabora (a very nice Greek goat milk cheese was made here), and in 1928 there was the connection of the railway to Mwanza on Lake Victoria. Here was the Steam Boat to various ports around the lake. At Bukoba, some school friends told me at night the hippos would come and graze before returning to the water during the day. Further on was the connection from Kalina to Mpanda, then ending up on the main line at Kigoma.

There was another railway line known as the Southern Province Railway (1949 to 1963), from Mtwara Harbour to Nachingwea to the end at Msasai. The train also stopped at Lindi Creek. I do not know much about this railway line, only it was connected with the Overseas Food Co-operation.

All I know is that in 1959 a friend of the family, Mr Bennett was murdered while organising the off-loading of a ship at the harbour.

Photos by Massow von Prince

# African Society

My experiences with the different people in Tanganyika amazed me. You see all these people dressed in their traditional way of their lives, such clothing, way of eating various ways of food, beliefs and religion.

I was born in a Lutheran Mission Hospital in the Usambara Mountains called Bumbuli. (I call myself a child of Africa.) Mother was operated on for a growth on the right breast and was unable to feed me so I was passed onto my wet nurse, Fatama. It was only natural that I would learn her language – Kishamba, then Swahili as I spent those first six years with Africans. The usual proverbiale white child being cared for by a nanny (*ayah*). Then at the age of five and a half I went to the Gillespie's farm, Masangula Estate, to learn English before going to Lushoto School.

When touring the Usambaras with friends years later (1979), we seemed lost when we came to some cross roads. Lucky for us, there just happened to be an African lady. We stopped, and I asked her in Swahili to indicate the road to Korogwe. The dear lady did not speak Swahili, so I had to wrack my brain from all those years ago, and then suddenly I could remember two words,

*Tete kaya* (Let's go home). So I said, "*Mimi tete kaya* – Korogwe" (I go home – Korogwe) and started a lot of hand pointing at the roads with a lot of language. Somehow I was understood, and the lady directed us to the road leading to Soni, then it was down to Mombo/Korogwe/Tanga on the main roads.

The Washamba ladies were always dressed beautifully with the colourful *kanga* (cloth). This cloth always has a saying written

# Tribal Homes

Masai

Built with cattle urine and dung. Walls wattle and roof also mud. Home in a thorn boma with cattle or in the open.

Wagogo

Wood and mud.
Thatch with wood and grass

Warusha

Built with mud and wattle. Thatch and Banana leaves.

Coastal Homes

Roof thatched with coconut fronds. Mud and wattle with an inclosed yard

Washamba

Corrugated or thatch roof. Brick or mud and wattle

in Swahili. It was like a sarong, wrapped around themselves and an extra cloth to cover their heads. Some women enjoyed having their ears pierced in rows of various sizes and the small rolls of different coloured paper discs attached to the outside of the ear lobe.

When a tourist ship came to Tanga, often a group of people went by coach to Lushoto to see the very colourful market. February was a very hot month on the coast as it was the month between the two rains (Short and the Monsoons), so a trip to Lushoto, being a small town up in the mountains, was a nice change from the heat of the coast.

On the sisal estate there were many tribes working, but I noticed the Makonde people who came from the Ruvuma River, south of Tanganyika/Mozambique area, had their homes built away from the other compounds where mixed tribes lived. The Makonde were good wood carvers. I once had a long wooden drum with a carved picture along the wood. At a *ngoma* the drum was placed between their legs near a fire which helped tighten the leather which gave a sharper tone. The *ngoma* was sometimes held by the house at Kulasi with dancing, music and singing. The Makonde tattooed their faces and bodies. The women would also have a wooden disc put into their pierced upper lip. Over the years I heard how the Makonde were liked on the sisal estates as they were hard workers, including the women would work in the fields with the men hoeing.

The sawmill was on the Umba River by Perani near the village of Mwakajembe on the Umba Steppe and river that leads on into Kenya and the sea. This river started to flow from the Usmbara Mountains. These people were good wood carvers in Kalambati – a little coloured sandal wood, or the very black or brown-black ebony hard woods.

About 1958/9 a young Masai Moran (worrier, Nilotic ethnic group) came visiting Tanga, and I noticed that he walked on his own on the pavement while the other people walked on the other side, away from him. Father mentioned that the Africans feared the raiding Masai, before colonization they would go right to the coast. It appears the fear was still there. The Masai were famous for their warring ways, and stealing of cattle before going back to their homeland.

When I was at Arusha School we were taken to see a Masai village. Their homes were made of mud, cattle manure and urine, using sticks to shape the homes with a semi-round flat roof, looking like a long loaf. When you stepped inside the floor was lower than the outside ground, and grown ups had to bend to get in. The floor was as if cement had been used, it was smooth and shiny. When you stepped inside there was a large clay pot with lovely clear water which was covered with a fresh leafy branch of a tree.

Another trip was to see how the Masai, being pastoral people, lived with their livestock. It was a huge *boma* (kraal) made from chopped thorn trees which kept them safe from marauding predators, such as lions, leopards, hyenas, wild dogs. Can you think of anything else, knowing the Masai was a feared people at the time? Watching the young Masai in their red loin cloth (*shuka*) tied over one shoulder, and around the waist a belt with an attached leather case to keep their two-sided long-flatted *machate* (panga) and a long spear. Metal to wood. Also, sometimes a long goud to use for their sour milk and blood mixed food. I was told for the young man had to prove his manhood after being circumcised. (This was done away from their homes and the women.) Their bodies were then covered with honey and as they lay down on the ground the young men had to endure the pain of the safari ants crawling over then. Their bodies were painted in red ochre and white paint. Their headdress was a long tapered stick and made up with attached string, then painted with red ochre and beads. Ears were also pierced and often had a brass ornament to hang to create a long lobe.

The Masai women in my time wore soft leather cloths which were beautifully embroided with beads. They also had beaded metal rings around their neck. The women had shaven head. I expect it was easier for them to have long leather ropes to place on their heads towards the front, this way it enabled them to carry firewood, water containers and other things.

Watching the young people dancing, especially the men with their very high leaping straight into the air and hearing the deep 'Ho ho' sound. The women with their *lala lala* made with flipping their tongue. This sound I only hear from women in Africa. I also was taught how to use the sound for joy.

With our trips out of school, we learnt a lot about the people living around us. So it was another trip to see the Mountain of God (Oldonyo Lengai) which was west of Arusha. The Masai believed that from this mountain which stood on its own, shaped like a cone, they could pray to God who lived in the sky. I could never understand as a child that their God was different to the Christian God, if everyone was praying to the sky which to me was heaven surely it was the same God. Oh well!!

Arusha had the Waarusha, and we were taken to their village where they lived at the foot hills of Mount Meru. Their homes were made round with sticks and mud. The roof was covered with lots of dried banana leaves. Unlike the Masai, they were agriculturalists, and lived in a forest of very tall bananas. From the dried leaves baskets could be made. There were a lot of hens around the homes. For our Cambridge exams I remembered the scenery, so used part of the subject given to us to paint a stormy day in Africa. Mine was this village in Arusha.

With one of the trips we did with Guides we went to Moshi and stayed at the Rectory, with its big veranda. While we were there we went to see the market and town where we noticed the Chaggas bring money in large money bags. We were told that the Chaggas did not trust paper money. The Chaggas normally farmed coffee, which Kilimanjaro is known for, also 25 different types of bananas.

Kongwa, what can I say? The Overseas Food Co-operation could not make a go in growing groundnuts. What happened to all those people who used to work there, I would not know. But the local tribe were the Wagogo. They were both herders and pastoral. These people were still encouraged to grow the groundnuts, but still could sell some of the crops to the OFC.

The hospital with all its top class equipment was turned into an African male nursing school as well as a hospital. One time they put on a show and we were able to go to see it. With lots of little acts, the one act was a joke against the local people, it went this way: *Peleka Wagogo Dodoma* (Please take the Wagogo to Dodoma). There was a mental asylum on Dodoma.

One year we heard the helicopters fly about, only to be informed that the Masai had raided the cattle from the Gogos. The police were late and the cattle were long gone into Masai land.

DOUBLE OUTRIGGER
NGALAWA
MTAMBWI
CANOE
MASHUA

# African Sailing Boats

When we came to live in Makindi – south of Tanga, Massow bought a 16 foot double outrigger sailing boat (*ngalawa*). Massow painted his boat black and named it *Sakarani*. Maragrete with help from an African made the canvas triangle sail. They cut the canvas to the right shape outside on the grass. Mother would sew the strips together on her Singer treadle sewing machine.

With me roaming about the area, we were living at the coast with mangrove swamps on the beach leading to the sea, and coconut trees on the land, I saw how the villagers lived. So it was, I came across some people making an outrigger boat from a very large felled mango tree. After the sides of the log had been burnt slightly, it seems to have been easier to use an Adze to chip away to shape the log into the haul. The Adze was like a hoe attached to a shaped stick at an angle. I never had the chance to see the finished boat.

When I was home one time, we had a trip in the outrigger. Heading to Pakamoyo, where the fish ponds were north of Tanga, but they soon realized that we would never make the return trip in time before sunset. The feel of the wind as we sailed along was a lovely feeling, with the sun and a few clouds. The boat was narrow and there was no sitting, so you just stood. One African stood on the one rigger holding a sail rope.

Massow needed a certain type of thick bamboo for a project he had in mind, so he sent the sailors off to Zanzibar to bring the bamboo back. On their return trip the one African standing on the rigger holding the sail rope dropped off to sleep, so the boat sank to their outrigger arms. An Arab dhow happened to sail by and recognized the name *Sakarani*, so they towed the boat back to Zanzibar, where our sailors could raise the boat for them to start the return trip back to Makindi.

The history as I read once, was that the outrigger boat originated from Philippines mainly centuries ago. These people sailed westward and the other countries to East Africa also copied the design. Some with only a single arm, but East Africa built with two riggers.

The fishermen sailed out very early in the morning to their fishing grounds, or to check their lobster pots, and then sail back to be at the beach about 13.00. To announce their return they would blow on a large conch shell (*kombe kubwa*). There was a man who made a hole at the small end of the shell. The sound carried well inland. The amazing thing was the villagers would be on the beach just as the boats arrived.

We often bought from them, especially the lobster which Mum would have walking on the kitchen floor until the bucket of water had boiled, then Mum would put the lobster head first into the water. In February the dhows (*jahazi*) would arrive before the monsoon rains, so would the eels coming from the Persian Gulf, along the East African coast. So great excitement. The 45 gallon drum would have two holes made at the side of the barrow, and a pipe would be threaded through. On this pipe the eel would be hung down. The open end of the barrow would be placed on three large rooks, where green coconut husks were lit. This created a slow smoke which was trapped inside the barrow. Next morning – hurray! We just loved smoked eel for breakfast. Also, sometimes a fisherman would bring us large black crabs, which Mother used to make a crab soup, or should I say *Pishi* Hassani would make it. Sometimes we bought shrimps from the Arab fishermen, who fished at night in their small dhows (*mash-uas*, a canoe style sailing boat) when the tide was out by the sand banks. They used lamps to attract the shrimps to their nets. The shrimps were boiled with a good quality silver spoon. If the spoon turned black, the shrimps found their way to the chicken run.

At the time the dhows (*jahazi*) arrived at the Tanga Harbour, we knew of their arrival. On the way to town on the Pangani road by the cemetery there were about six Arab homes. These Arabs traded in dry shark meat from the Persian Gulf. Boy the smell from the fresh stock! You had to be there to experience the delight of this experience.

During the spring and nip tides, it was a good time to walk on the sand banks and among the coral reef and see all the creatures and vegetation, the water was so shallow. You had to weae Bata *takkies* (tennis shoes or plimsolls). The reason was often people would get a prick from the sea urchins with long spines and that would cause a lot of pain and often it was not easy to pull out the spine, so one had to just wait for it to make its way out a week or so later. The other creature to watch out for were the clams. Sometimes a person would stand on an open clam and it clamped his foot, and the only way to release the foot was to make a fire above the clam and the heat of the water would force the clam to open up so you could get your foot out. A story I heard from the Africans. When the tide was low, the fishermen would also check their lobster pots, and add more seaweed in the basket.

One could see the odd giant fossil clam shell jutting out on the cliffs. We had two of these shells. Father donated one to the Pietermaritzburg Museum when they moved to South Africa.

Another way to catch fish was to build a high fence with poles in a V shape trap. Fish were trapped when the tide went out. The end side of the trap was shaped like a bowl where the fisherman could then collect the fish. There was no escape for the bigger fish.

On the other side of the mangrove swamp going south from the cliffs, one would pass an old Arab grave yard. Then you came out onto a creek. Here the Africans had their sea salt making open sheds. There was a long metal tray filled with sea water during the low tide period. Underneath the metal tray they had a lot of coconut husks which were lit which gave a slow heat. With the heat, the water would evaporate. Next day the salt would be left to dry. It was crystal pure white salt. Nothing like sea salt for taste.

I must not forget to mention a time Bridget Goodrich (Chip) and I took a very old canoe (*mtumbi*) with holes and its two poles. As the tide was high, we could go poling among the mangrove trees. Lucky we had some chewing gum and we stuffed the old hole with it. We must have spent an hour there. One could also see the small crabs climbing up the long roots of the mangrove trees as well as the climbing fish, known as mudskippers, an amphibian fish, you could see the front side fins used like feet to climb the roots, trees. They could also jump about.

Father also made a raft with 45 gallon drums. This was used to collect old dead coral near the side of the mangrove on the sea side. The Africans would dig up the coral, which was then placed on the raft waiting for the tide to lift the raft up, and with a pole we would push the raft along to the beach. This coral was left in a huge pile on the land for about ten years to allow the rain water to wash the salt out. Dad mentioned that the cement would not stick well when building as the salt would not hold the cement together. He also collected the beach sand and had it on the land for the rain to wash out the salt.

Dad designed the coral house, which is now part of a holiday resort.

A common sight in the rainy season.

# Cars and lorries

With the age of steam, our horses and cart were slowy phased out to be turned into vehicles still using the word horsepower. Cars made it easier for people to travel long distances, which, I must say suited me very well.

My parents had a wonderful Ford Box Body in the 1940s. I forget what model it was, though Mother did tell me once.

Those wonderful roads in Africa depending on the season, which meant us travelling in the dry season on dusty, corrugated, bumpy, potholed roads. This was ideal for us young people. Speed was maintained to fly over the corrugation on the road to make it more comfortable, but should Dad or Mum hit a bump, then to my delight the Ford went flying in the air. (Lovely!) Oh! I must not forget the dust, especially in areas where the soil was so-called red. It was not easy to overtake the cars in front as the dust was too thick.

Now the rainy season, especially the monsoon time, with rains on the coast falling for about three months, not to forget the short rains of December/January. We often travelled with a Tuni Boy (assistant), with such tools, spade, panga, small axes, all to help dig the vehicle out of the mud when you got stuck. Cutting branches to place in front of the car to a point the car could grip the road again. We all had to get out and help. During those very heavy rains we also used chains wrapped around the wheels.

Going to Morogoro to get onto the school train to go to Kongwa. The stretch of road from Korogwe, Handeni with its deep red soil, we would often see Railway bus, on its side and other vehicles having got stuck in the mud. One year we had the problem of being stuck and we had to get off the Railway bus and give a little push.

As we had a sisal estate up to 1948, in 1949 after my sister Frederica was born we moved to Tanga, Makindi was five miles south of Tanga on the cliff top overlooking the sea. In the lorries we had our belongings, plus belongings of any Africans and their families who were coming with us to Tanga.

But I must not forget the 20 plus/minus cats we had that were put into hessian sacks. Plus my lovely black cat, Horsery.

At Perani near Mwakajembi by the Kenya border and on the Umba River, Dad started sawmilling. Dad stayed at the mill setting it up with old steam boilers to drive other machinery, using a pully and vee belts drive system. Mother stayed at home in Makindi, where we had sheds to stock the sawn timber, and from there sold the timber. Mother communicated with Father weekly, bringing supplies and the wages.

During the time we had the sawmill in Perani, the lorry drivers would stop at one of the villages to buy food and the driver was told all were aboard except the one African who was climbing using the wheel. When the vehicle moved forward, the poor man got caught and moved with the wheel forward and was crushed to death.

European people living along the coast from Mwambani village to us, wanted electricity, so my parents were asked to transfer the sawmill to Makindi from Perani as it would make it more viable to bring the electricity to this area, and having a factory helped to reduce the cost for the private homes.

Lorries were needed now to bring logs out of the forests to the mill. One year we had an army Bedford lorry, and father's friend Rolf Bennett (they met in camp in South Africa), came often to visit, but one time Mr Bennett striped the Bedford lorry to service it, and I had to be part of the grease monkey team. It does help to learn about the engine. Also Dad had various Europeans working for him – Like Danny Nortjie, Mr Rigas, and an Italian (forgot his name). Also a Sikh whose child came with me, Thomas and Uta to school in Tanga when I went to work in the morning.

Other lorries were the Commer and Thames. Also they had numerous (Beetle) Volkswagen and a short-base Land Rover, with which I learnt to drive. Mother was my instructor.

During the drivers' strike in 1959, I had to learn to drive a lorry. We needed to take the sawdust away. Mr Singh would go very early in the morning to the forest to bring the logs back to the factory, and in the afternoon I did when I came back from work with Thomas and Uta (my brother Hanson's children) from school. The workers would fill the lorry with sawdust which had wooden sides, and it was a job to drive this through deep coastal sandy soil and in and out of the coconut trees. As you know the trees are not all that straight.

Many a time in that two-week strike Father would let me know how many trees I had scraped the side of the lorry with. The sawdust we took to the African coconut plantations and spread it out on the ground between the trees.

One good thing about that strike was that I really learnt how to double clutch when changing the gears. When I learnt to drive I had to get to know the engine of the Land Rover, change types, etc.

*Motor Rallies of East Africa, Tanga*

The coconut plantation growing in and around the old airfield was where sporting cars came from all over East Africa to compete in the local race. I went to this show with my first boyfriend. I was naive and stupid as I wanted to look good. I wore my first pair of high heels that I had as a Christmas present from my parents. Well!

Then came the East African Safari which started from Nairobi – Kenya and went on to Kampala – Uganda, then crossing over to Tanganyika having gone to Dar es Salaam then up to Tanga. Then driving through the Usambara Mountains and down to the coast and on to Mombassa – Kenya, and back to Nairobi.

I had joined the Tanga Special Constabulary and our work at this time was to handle the police radio connecting Tanga to Nairobi passing on information on the progress to the vehicles on their way to Kenya. That was 1958.

In 1959 I went with Dick and Renee Blackway to Handeni to help manage that rally stop, reporting to Tanga by radio who had come by and were on their way again. This was a little different from the Police Station in Tanga.

The East African Safari was started in 1953 and was known as the Coronation Safari as part of Queen Elizabeth's coming to the throne. It was held over the Easter Holidays. The weather was very mixed as it was also in the rainy season.

*Airport – Motor racing*

By the airport and what was once the old runway. There was still tar on the ground among the coconut trees. It was here the motor racing track was set up. I was invited by a friend to join and watch, this was soon after I left school. The competitors in their racing cars came from Nairobi, Dar es Salaam, and Mombasa. I do not remember who else was there.

Tanga airport was a single storey building. The East African Airways looked after this airport. At times I would go to my friends who worked in the watchtower and watch the Dakota DC3 arriving and taking off.

One year I went to Dar es Salaam for my local leave and flew via Zanzibar. The landing was not too good and you could smell the burnt tyres. The air hostess said the pilot was drunk.

My husband and I flew to Zanzibar in 1961 in the same type of plane, when we came on a visit from the Federation of Rhodesia and Nyasaland.

Tanga harbour and sea

# Tanga

My home town from 1948/9 to 1960.

The family moved from the Korogwe area of the Lwengera Valley. Soon after Frederica was born the family moved to Mwambani, an area called Makindi about 5/7 miles south of Tanga, by the sea. Our home was an old Arab type house on five acres. It was the last residence on the cliff next to the mangrove forest.

No sooner were we settled when Mother said the locals came to claim compensation for the mango and coconut trees, saying that the trees belonged to them, though they were part of the property. Oh, well!

The house had two rooms. One was their bedroom and the other the lounge and office, divided by a passage. The front had a wide veranda. The inner courtyard also had verandas as part of the main building, here was the dining room and where I had my bed when I was home, and off this were three rooms. One was the washroom where the RED LAND CRABS lived, the other two rooms were used as store rooms. To the north side, a door opened to the outside. Here Dad had an open plan kitchen with a store to the back. To the south side there was an open garage, then a big room with partly enclosed verandas. Outside this building was another building with two rooms and a passage dividing them. Like in Kulasi the bath was a large concrete bath, the other was the dressing room; also the toilet. Behind this building was an open laundry. I also remember the windmill to generate power (a common sight on farms in Africa and Australia). That was before we had electricity. The hot water was boiled in a 45 gallon oil drum built on an enclosed brick stand, with an opening at the bottom where timber was placed and lit to heat the water. The water was then carried in buckets to the bath.

Years later, in 1960/61 father built his Coral House, by then I had left for Rhodesia.

The parents started developing the property. Building more buildings for staff and sheds to house the timber coming from Perani Sawmill. The ground was ancient coral sea beds. This could be seen as from the edge of the cliffs along the coast Dad retrieved two huge prehistoric clam shells. One he gave to the museum in Pietermaritzburg, South Africa. Massow had a huge hole dug to use the soil as foundations for the buildings. This hole was lined with cement and then covered with corrugated sheets. Rain water from the homestead was directed to this storage area. By this water tank was a borehole that fed the house with running water.

When Perani Sawmill was transferred to Makindi, as the other residents along the cliff towards Mwambani village, approached Father to have his mill here as the Electricity Board would only bring electricity if they had some sort of industry to make it more worthwhile. This second hole, the earth was used for the foundation for the mill building and base for the machinery to stand on. Then it was filled with water for Mother's muscovy ducks (*Cairina moschata*). Margarete managed to breed her ducks to have a black patch on the head like a hat, and the rest pure white feathers.

As I mentioned, our new home was an old Arab house. If you took a walk south of the cliff and at the bottom, by the beach there were three Tamarind trees by the beach. This was the start of the mangrove swamp. It was here I would also see the Africans bring their boats if they needed mending. Anyway walking between the mangrove trees and the grassland, one came across old Arab graves. You can see some of them had been studded with mineral stones. This path would take me to a creek where the Africans had their sea salt making sheds. On the north side of the house on the cliff there was a huge baobab tree. Makes one wonder what the trade was – I used to wonder.

A grouter was dug out at the lower side of the cliff when we walked down to the beach. This big pool was near the house with very sweet water. We also had a borehole, but this water was brackish. A South African man came and dowsed with a forked stick from a mulberry tree. He said the mulberry tree had a good connection to underground streams.

Some of the land was sold and we had neighbours like Renata Zimmerman married to Dick Blakeway who worked for the Volkswagen Motor company. She had a lovely collection of orchids. There were the Harridge family, they had a dress shop in Tanga and Arusha. Then Major Falkner with his wife. She used to collect things for Kew in London. I saw some of her works at the Herbarium in Salsibury (Harare), Rhodesia.

## Amboni Sisal Estate and Caves

Sisal was introduced to German East Africa from the Americas. The German company had its headqarters in Dusseldorf, Germany. After World War One German property was expropriated by the British. But one of the directors was Swiss and he told the Authorities that Dusseldorf was a small village in Switzerland. This company was administered by Swiss people in my time in Tanga. I used to come with the parents to meet up with Dr and Mrs Seitz. They left Germany before World War Two. His wife was a Catholic Jew, and they came to Tanga as a medical doctor for the Amboni Estate.

The estate was north of Tanga on the road leading to Mombasa, Kenya. From the Sietz home, you could look south across the mangrove swamps to Toten Island in Tanga Bay and harbour.

We often visited and one time when I was 14 years old, I spent a week with Dr and Mrs Seitz, where Mrs Seitz taught me how to perform in the upper class way of life. One of the lessons was the laundry. Washing the clothes for the men, you had to use extra soap, rubbing it on the neck and underarm, as the men sweat a lot, before putting it into the washing machine. Also Mrs Seitz said one should not wear the clothes bought, as often in the factories when the garments were made there were a lot of sick people and one could pick up their diseases. Then the next lesson was how to set a table for a very special dinner and dance. Well, my dancing was not good. We had two young men for dinner and then the dancing after dinner when one of the men would come and ask me to dance and how to accept and go onto the dance floor in the correct manner. Something one never forgets.

We went with the young people to the estate club house, where there was a skittle alleyway. This was fun. I had the wrong dress as the sleeves split from part of the dress.

About 12 miles from Tanga was the Galanos Sulpher Springs near the Mombasa road which crossed the Zigi (Ziggi) River. Mrs Seitz took me there when there was a wooden hut on the edge of the springs, and it was here Mrs Seitz would change into a swimming costume and sit in the sulphur water for a while.

On the same road to Mombasa about 8 miles from Tanga, are the Amboni Caves. Father took us to see. The guide lit a long reed rush in a bundle and led us to the near caves. These caves are from the time of the Jurassic period, about 150 million years. The place was rough looking with a lot of bush around. It was an amazing place, with lots of caves. I have no idea how far they go in.

## Mzesani/Lazoni – Ralli Brothers Estates

With the Suez Crisis in 1956, Massow lost his contract and market of flooring blocks to Europe and the UK with the Liverpool-Uganda Company. Father had to find something else to do to keep his sawmill working, so he turned to furniture making and camp doors for housing on sisal estates. So he went to Mzesani to cut timber. The trees were of various hard woods. It was also the time Massow acquired a Bedford Army lorry, as it was needed with its four-wheel drive to get into the forest during the rainy season, to bring the logs out. During the rains the Beetle was best as it could be pushed along the deep ruts. I often went with Dad and stayed with the manager, Klaus von Ungern-Sternburg and his wife Ulli and daughter Irene, during the school holidays. My friendship stayed well after school.

I enjoyed being at the estate with the young people. There was tennis, hockey and other minor sports, even when I left school. Sometimes Prince Eisenberg's daughter joined us. Ulli was helping her with her health, as she had the latest massage equipment.

Mjesani Sisal Estate Mill is by the Sigi (Zigi/Ziggi) River near the rapids, where the river was wide and with high banks on either side with a bridge across.

The country was changing and we noticed the odd strike going on. We had a drivers' strike. But once I was in Mjesani when the workers went on strike and they decided to cross the bridge converging onto the administration buildings. The police were there to help protect the administrative staff. It was a really angry crowed and very frightening. A police officer fired into the air with his gun to holt the works, but they panicked and the people in front turned back, but others were still coming across the bridge, so you can guess. The bridge was blocked with people and with this turn around some people fell over the bridge to their death. After this the policeman was demoted and sent to a remote town in the south of Tanganyika.

I was again at the British Library seeing maps and reading, and in one of the articles I noticed that 31 German-owned sisal estates were taken over as enemy property, which included Lazoni and Mjesani. These estates were advertised for sale by the government in England as well as Tanganyika. The Ralli Brothers must have taken their chance to purchase the estate. I was told they had rubber plantation in Indonesia. This knowledge came from an elderly lady I once looked after her as a carer in 1992. She was connected to the Ralli family

## Pangani – road south of Tanga

This road took us to Makindi. On the way out we went over the railway line. This divided the town. Once over the railway the road to the west was to the go-downs along the railway, today known as the industrialist estate. To the opposite side of the road, east was the housing for the working people.

Not far out on the right hand side, heading south was the huge cemmtary and it was here the police rifle range was. On the left of the road were about 6/8 Arab homes. These people dealt with the sale of dried fish, mainly shark meat. When there was a sudden fresh smell of the fish, you knew the dhows had arrived from the Persian Gulf, usually in February, ahead of the monsoon rains. The dhows usually anchored on the west side of the harbour (it was the time that the eels also arrived from the north).

It is an interesting road, as you pass a big village, where one can buy your beef on Sunday, as it was the day a beast was killed. This was confirmed when I met a man working at the Bodleian Library, Oxford. He was from that village.

About half way down to Pangani, an old Arab trading place with old ruins of a town, was a family we would sometimes visit on the sisal estate. On one such a day having lunch the parents of the young boywere speaking French to him. Apparently it was his French week. The parents had other weeks for English and German. The other language we all spoke to the Africans was Kiswahili.

Once when we arrived in Pangani, we would visit another German family. This very old town must have been an ancient trading harbour. The Pangani River is wide and deep and can allow bigger boats to go up and anchor. On the south side of the river was a very high cliff. On the north side of the river was the town, and beyond coconut plantations. Here Mr WI Tame had a home and kept his sea-going yacht here. The family once invited me and we set out towards Pemba Island. We went round to the east side of the island. Here were huge dunes of white sand. It was beautiful. The Grundys also lived here and they had a workshop making things from wrought-iron, not just tables or lamps but gates, also the Tanga Library gates. Mr Grundy had a boat for transporting goods between Zanzibar, Tanga and Pangani.

One day we were with the District Administrator (DA) and he spoke of his time in Malaysia doing the same job there. To overcome complaints of people stealing crops, he would use four bottles with some liquid, these were placed one each to the four corners of the property, and get a witch doctor to put a spell on the bottles to stop the thieving. He used the same method in Pangani. It did the trick. It protected the property and the coconuts were not stolen. The gentleman whose name I have forgotten, showed Dad an old German cannon he had found walking on the high cliff. He did not know how it worked, so Father showed him. What a bang.

I would like to mention that without the help of the British Library, getting permission from the Minitry of Defence to get a map of Pangani would have been impossible. I was able to have a more detailed map, where up the river there was a waterfall and dam which supplied the energy for the Hydro system. In my time it also supplied energy to Mombasa, Kenya.

## Police – Special Constabulary

The year I left school in 1957 the Police Special Constabulary was formed and I joined. It was fun and new friends. We were taught how to handle the radio system, road speeding calculations with the stop watch and radio with the other police down the road informing on the speeding driver, who was stopped.

We were being instructed for a Government driving licence. As usual my left and right hand never really knew where to turn. The instructor would say 'turn left', I would then turn right. Ha Ha. We were shown how to study the engine. Very useful if the vehicle stalled etcetera. This knowledge I found useful during our Bush War in Rhodesia. I helped many women who could not get their car started, even our car the Humber Super Snip. I also changed a tyre for a lady with her child who did not have a spare or know how to change it. She was heading home to one of the game parks where her husband had his job. I just happened to come across her on the road on my way back from Salisbury.

Another training we had at the rifle range. The ground was in part of the cemetery. The weapons we used were the .303 rifle, I was not too good with this gun. Then, the pistol, same story not too good. But the best of all was the Tommy gun firing from the hips. When I was married there was a snake in the hen house, and the gardener called me, so no problem I fetched the 12 bore gun. I had never used one before. Well, I took aim and pulled the trigger, killed the snake, but I did not know how it kicked, and I fell flat backwards onto the floor. I was praised as a good shot. After that I used the gun in the same way as in the film *Annie Get Your Gun* from the hips.

To join the other people at the rifle range for our practise, the police sent a vehicle to fetch me and I would then have breakfast with these lovely young men at the Police Mess. My father soon put a stop to me taking part, even not to go back to the Police.

I missed that as we had become friends, and often met at the little club that had formed. It was there that we got paid our One Shilling for the day's work. I really enjoyed my time there. Oh well!

## Working

My parents arranged my first job and that was working for Lehmann Limited, the headquarters was in London, with another branch in Dar es Salaam. It was a hardware company and I was a typist. My shorthand was not very good. I would rather have worked for Collins, the bookkeeper's office. I did bookkeeping for my Cambridge exams. This job suited my parents well, as I would take Tom and Uta to school and return home for lunch. As it was just a half day job my wages were SH30.00 per month.

Pity I do not remember my boss's name. He was a tall dark haired man, who loved to smoke his curved pipe, which hung down his chin, not the straight kind. He had a special drawer with all the equipment, such as tobacco cleaning tool, tobacco in a pouch, and a lighter. Often one could hear the frustration when the tobacco would not light.

Mr Khatri in the accounts department taught me how to do 100% short cuts. Very useful to me in my later life.

I also worked in the afternoons at Wigglesworth and Company. This company handled the marketing of various crops, but mainly sisal from before World War Two. Always, I battled with shorthand and spelling. I still have my small Collin's dictionary.

From The National Archives in Kew, I came across an article stating that R Lehmanns & Co did the export of Papain to America in 1952. As mentioned earlier we had a paw paw plantation in Magoma on the sisal estate.

My boss was known to help people and their health. One lady was dying and he helped drain the pain from her body, so she passed away peacefully.

## Friends and Family

The Goodricks lived the other side of Mwambani village by the sea. They were four girls. Biddy (Chip) and I spent time together sometimes, her younger sister Doreen was more Frederica's age. We lived about 5 miles away from each other. The story mother told me, was she left Fidi with her friend while Mum went into town. When she got back home, thinking Fidi was safe with her friends, she found these two girls in her bedroom with her powder spread around her bedroom. These two girls had walked through the coconut plantation on their own. I also used to do that when visiting that side of the village. One time on such a trip, I saw an African with his nose cut off. I was told there were two of them, but one died, this chap survived. Their punishment for stealing coconuts.

Then later the Cluers came to live there and they had two boys, Douglas and Nigel, who became friends with my brother's children Tom and Uta. Olga and Roderick (Rod) had sailed from England to East Africa via the Suez with their two very small children in their 60 foot minesweeper ship, ending up at Mafia Island. Before coming to Tanga they sold their ship.

At the Bodleian Library looking up information of Massow's use of timber, I came across Rod's name with his coir factory and business.

The von Prince and Cluer children went to the same school in Tanga, and from this friendship I became friends with the family. They would take me with them sometimes in their cabin cruiser to go goggle fishing out to the reefs. One time the Cluers had invited some sailors who had arrived with their naval ship from Arabia, and we were coming back to shore in the evening when we realised I was guiding the boat towards a ship that was in harbour. A crash was avoided. Wonderful to have such experienced people on board.

Through the Cluers I met my husband Wilfred, Olga's brother.

There was Mrs Childs who worked on African violets cross-breeding them to get different colours. She had a wonderful collection and she pointed out one or two had her name attached to the colour she had created.

Renee Zinnette married Dick Blakewell. He managed the Volkswagen Company. They were our neighbours and I joined her company at a party at the Sisal Growers' Hall. Renee grew the most beautiful orchids. One time they went on a long holiday and asked me to look after her plants. When they came back Renee was surprised how the plants had grown. The reason partly was Renee's was always feeling the plants and I just left them alone. I have seen that with crops, when machinery went over plants all the time like at crop spraying time, or the path of the tractor, the plants stay small.

Tanga Harbour and Yacht Club, one can see the Toten Island.

## Tanga by the sea

Tanga is an interesting town surrounded by a bay with the Toton Island in the middle opposite the harbour, yacht club and the swimming area. And not far to the east the hospital built during the German period. From there the road takes you to Raskazone residential area. During the German time there was a coconut plantation.

The town itself was laid out by the Germans with big teak trees on the main street where the post office was and it was the main shopping area. Also not far from this centre going to Raskazone was the embankment cut away taking you down to the harbour. From the post office going north along the coast you came to the various government buildings and the library, and junior school. But there was open area looking towards Toton Island and a ship that had been sunk. I was told later that an Italian salvage company had removed the ship in the end. But that view was part of the Sea View Hotel owned by the Progulas family. Helen and her brother were also at Kongwa School. The Progulas family had another hotel callled the Africa Hotel and it was known as the gambling hotel, where people could easily have a complete change of homes. Like a whole sisal estate could be lost at the tables.

As you move away from the sea, you go westward to other businesses like Lehmanns facing a park, opposite was Riddock garage and other hardware shops. Also going to the open air

Tanga town

market. Then another hotel and the railway station. The Go-downs.

The main roads leading to or from Tanga: one going to Mombasa, Kenya to the north, or westward to Arusha and Moshi. Then southward to Pangani. The trains went to Arusha, on the railway line that went to Korogwe, the west side of the Usambara Mountains. South a road led to Pangani and in the dry season from Pangani you crossed the river to a road along the coast line to Bagamoyo and then Dar es Salaam. During the rains with its black cotton soil it was impossible for vehicles to pass.

Tanga was a colourful town with its diversity of people. I always thought of the tall elegant Somali women in their beautiful gentle colour long dresses. The Swahili ladies in their colourful *kanga*, while the men wore the long white *kanzu* or for everyday wear, a sarong. The Indian ladies in their beautiful elegant saris. The Sikh men with their turbans. Arabs or Muslim women in their day wear of hijab and scarfs, either with their faces sometimes covered, but always a scarf to hide their hair. The men in their cloaks, and dagger on a belt across their front.

When a tourist ship called, there was a coach which took tourists up to Lushoto to see the market with all the beautiful ladies in their colourful *kangas*.

In other words we had a hugely diverse community. Though English and Kiswahili were the main languages, one heard various European, African and Asian spoken langauges.

Makindi: The Arab House with additions

Makindi: The Arab House with additions

Massow, Margarete Massowia, Frederica

Thomas and Uta (1955)

Fidi, Massowia and Juma

Porcupine. We had two but a witchdoctor killed one for medicine.

Soft nose Dik Dik

Michael Zanzibar Donkey

Mother's Muscovy Duck with a black hat

# My Last Few Years in Tanganyika

Who would know that I would end up going to the Federation of Rhodesia and Nyasaland in 1960.

Through my friendship with the Cluers, I met Olga's brother, Wilfred Haywood. The first time was at an evening in 1958 at the Sisal Growers' Association Hall. When a strange man asked for a dance, I just ran away. The second time was a year later, 1959, at the Cluer's home. I liked the man. On Wilfred's return to Rhodesia by ship, when he arrived in Beira. he sent a telegram proposing marriage; in fact it was two which I accepted.

Wilfred returned in January 1960 and in February we married. We did a little traveling together to the Ngorongoro Crater. After our little trip we made our way to the Federation of Rhodesia and Nyasaland.

Olga asked me what I thought of Wilfred's Humber Super Snipe. I said he should have bought a Mercedes-Benz as it was better for the rough roads at the time.

It was the rainy season, which which made the roads hard to drive as there were no tarmac roads. Our road took us from Tanga via Korogwe, Morogoro and Iringa. Here we stopped to have the brake pipe seen too, as the rocks on the road had made a hole in the fuel pipe. The same happened again in Mbeya. We were now on the Great North Road,

The car was fine when we got to the border of Tunduma, Tanganyika (Tanzania) and Nakonde, Northern Rodesia (Zambia). Now we were on roads that were heavy going due to the rains and the muddy red soil until we got to about Kampiri Mposhi, when the roads improved heading towards Lusaka, but still no brakes. We were lucky we did not get stuck on the road like other vehicles, also lorries.

Wilfred told me to drive through Lusaka and its traffic lights. It was my first time driving with traffic lights to the Rootes

Group garage for the Humber. From then on it was driving on tarmac roads to Gatoma (Kadoma), crossing at Kafue (Zambia), Chirundo (Zimbabwe) on to Salisbury (now Harare). Then to my new home on the farm.

What struck me was how different the people were to East Africans. The country did not feel cheerful. The country had signs in public places: Whites or Blacks Only. I was shocked when I walked into the post office and the lady would not serve me as I was in the Blacks Only section. I remember saying that in six month's time the blacks would go on strike. It happened.

www.ingramcontent.com/pod-product-compliance
Lightning Source LLC
Chambersburg PA
CBHW022010080426
42733CB00007B/545
*9781914245381*